THIRTY CHIC DAYS

Practical inspiration for a beautiful life

FIONA FERRIS

ISBN-13: 978-1523670031
ISBN-10: 1523670037

For Paul, my one and only

Book Bonuses

http://bit.ly/ThirtyChicDaysBookBonuses

Click on or type in the link above to receive your free special bonuses.

'21 ways to be chic' is a fun list of chic living reminders, with an MP3 recording to accompany it so you can listen on the go as well.

You will also **receive a subscription** to Fiona's blog '*How to be Chic*', for weekly inspiration on living a simple and beautiful French-inspired life.

Contents

Prologue

If you're anything like me, you've read every French chic book and blog out there. Although it's a somewhat saturated market, I still read everything I come across because I find there's always a new angle or something fresh to enhance my life; simply absorbing another person's thoughts on a subject can spark off a new enthusiasm.

For me, I love the fanciful thoughts of being more chic and 'French' but I also love the practical aspect. It's all very well dreaming of living in an elegant apartment in the second arrondissement, but most of us live in a normal house or condo with a view of the neighbours, rather than the Eiffel Tower.

Don't let that stop you though; why not choose to view your everyday life through a French-tinted filter? As far as we know, we only have this one life, so let's make it fun and enjoyable. All that's needed is a little imagination plus a belief in our ability to create and live our lives the way we want to.

In *Thirty Chic Days* you will find easy, instantly applicable ideas to elevate your day-to-day life. There's no need to run away to Paris when you can bring a feeling of the City of Light to you right now, exactly where you are.

Introduction

Many of us have a long-distance love affair with France, and, in particular, with the Parisian woman. However, we don't want to be an exact copy of her, rather, we want to be *our own interpretation* of her – a chic, polished version of ourselves really, as we go about our day.

I truly believe any woman can be chic if she wants to be and it is not restricted to those of French birthright. Yes, there are some fortunate creatures to whom it all comes effortlessly, then there are those of us who want to know 'how it works'; those of us who adore all things pretty and stylish, who have made it a life-long quest to work out how to be our chicest selves... in a relaxed and easy manner, of course.

We have lots going on in our lives every single day, but we still like to carry ourselves with an air of *panache* and style.

There are many simple changes you can apply day-by-day which will transform your life. You can live in a more elegant and chic way right now, starting today if you want.

Some folk are motivated to move their entire lives to France, immersing themselves in the culture, the language and the way of life. For the rest of us, Paris feels more like a beautiful daydream.

We may well like the place where we live, love being close to family and friends; we even enjoy our chosen occupation, or at least the paycheck we bring home. That's very French you know – 'work to live', not 'live to work'.

The rest of the time, when we're not earning a living, we can make our lives everything we wish them to be, with a little inspiration and the courage to choose to live the way we've always dreamed of.

What does 'chic' mean to you?

Over time I have come to rely less on the mythical ideal French woman, instead working out what 'chic' means to me. I still read widely on the subject, but I know myself well enough now to recognise what I want in life – I can discern which parts I say 'yes' to and which parts I reject as not right for me.

There are many ways we can create *je ne sais quoi* for ourselves. From the French, *je ne sais quoi* literally means 'I don't know what', but more colloquially means 'that certain something'. Wikipedia describes the phrase as 'an intangible quality that makes something or someone distinctive or attractive'.

Finding chic motivation via inspiration is the best way to go: making yourself so excited that you cannot *not* do those things that you previously wished you could be bothered to do. You'll find the more you do something, the more you want to do it, so you start gaining a great forward momentum. Yes, sometimes that momentum drops off, often after the initial novelty and enthusiasm falls away, but you can keep it going by reminding yourself of the payoff, of why you wanted to live this way in the first place.

You may decide to read *Thirty Chic Days* all at once to begin with, or you may choose to dip into different chapters (or 'days') as they appeal to you. It is my sincere wish in writing this book that you find many inspiring, useful ideas to put into practice both straight away, as well as in the future. Many of these ideas do not require you to spend money, indeed it is often what you take away from your life rather than add that will help you to cultivate a chic way of being.

Keep a tiny notebook or notepad and pen with you to jot down ideas you want to try. I hope this book is like an encouraging friend who wants the best for you; a friend who wants you to live a full, rich, healthy, happy life.

Read on to find out how you can bring excitement, fun and *joie de vivre* ('joy of living') to your life, starting today.

Day 1
Have a Paris state of mind

I may not live in a Paris apartment (and I don't live in France, or even Europe), but I certainly go through my day as if I do. It can be easy to find life a little humdrum at times so, just for fun, I dress in the morning as if I am skipping off to catch the Metro to work, when in reality, my husband and I are travelling along a suburban street in our shared Toyota.

Even though I am more than happy and content, I still love dreaming about being my ideal French girl living a chic and stylish life. I may be working on my computer or lining up at the bank but, in my mind, I am living in Paris, skipping along narrow Montmartre streets in my high heels to pick up a warm baguette from the *boulangerie*.

I decorate on my small budget as if I live in an elegant Parisian abode. When I am shopping for dinner ingredients I imagine I am in a French *supermarché* rather than our local grocery store. I flick through the clothes on my hangers at home as if I'm browsing in my favourite St-Germain-des-Prés boutique.

Carrying out my daily routine with a sprinkling of French fantasy helps me make better choices most of the time; happily, that good feeling continues because there is no remorse as there can be with other less helpful 'feel-good' activities such as snacking on chocolate.

If I am less than motivated when shopping for dinner ingredients, I ask myself questions such as 'what would I choose to cook if I was living in my dream Paris apartment?', 'what would my French girl be doing right now?' or 'how would my Parisian self handle this?'

The simple act of asking questions such as these sets the brain clicking over, which means I am easily able to change my course of thinking towards the desired direction. I can act as if I am the chic French woman of my dreams and all is well again.

Yes, it's pretending, but I prefer to look at it as a minor course correction – an enjoyable one – which gets me back on the right path, that lovely cobbled lane with cafes and bistro tables either side.

Act as if

You may have heard the great advice that says 'dress for the job you want, not the job you have'? Well, *acting as if* goes along with that. Pretending you are the person you want to be actually helps you become that person.

I know my mythical Parisienne may not even exist, but that's not the point; the point is whatever inspires me, inspires me. I freely admit that my French girl is entirely idealised and serves no other purpose than to encourage me to be my best. I take my favourite elements of the idealistic Parisian life and tailor them to suit me. Why not elevate my day-to-day life by dreaming then doing? I can then be a touch more chic and elegant while running my necessary errands.

Rather than try to *motivate* myself to do something, I find it much easier to *inspire* myself to do that same thing; having a chic headspace does that for me. When I imagine I am a sophisticated French woman preparing for her day, I am inspired to iron a blouse, rather than go for the wash-and-wear option.

Imagine sitting down to eat dinner in your petite, minimal Paris apartment; would you pull a tray of pre-cooked fries and nuggets from the oven to smother with tomato sauce, washing it all down with diet cola?

Or would it be nicer to think about pottering in your kitchen putting together a plate of hot-smoked salmon, micro-greens with a sprinkle of home-made vinaigrette, and a slice of baguette accompanied by a goblet of sparkling mineral water?

Imagine you are meeting your lover for lunch at a café in Paris's 8th arrondissement. Surely you will choose a tasty, healthful salad with freshly grilled chicken in preference to a plate of nachos made with corn chips, greasy beef and beans, and a huge dollop of sour cream with melted cheese covering the lot. You want to feel sexy and desirable when meeting your date, not like a greedy hoovering piglet. Even if you were dining by yourself, surely it would be a preferable way to feel.

When I first travelled to Paris fifteen years ago, I had lunch at a café on the Champs Élysée which didn't *feel* like a total tourist trap, but it probably was. I remember that I ordered an omelette and cappuccino for lunch, which felt elegantly Parisian. I still remember my lunch with great fondness simply because it anchored me into my ideal French girl mindset.

Other ways to *act as if*

To stand up for yourself, act as if you are more **confident** than you already are. You will then start to *feel* more confident as you make decisions from that place.

To become **slimmer**, act as if you already are svelte, making slim-person food choices, identifying with slender people rather than overweight ones. Go into your kitchen and look around as if you were visiting. Ask yourself what kind of a person lives here? Would a slim lady have *this* in her pantry or fridge?

If you are overwhelmed with many tasks to undertake, act as if you are the most **organised, charming** person in the world, completing everything with grace and ease.

If you come home after work tired and grumpy, ready to pour the wine and blob, act as if you are **motivated and chic**, putting away whatever you've brought in with you, tidying up, changing into your loungewear, starting dinner and pouring yourself a glass of sparkling mineral water.

In the morning if you are feeling too lazy to iron a cotton shirt, even though you love the look, act as if you are your ideal French girl, **breezily ironing in her Paris apartment** (with lavender-scented air coming in the metal-framed windows overlooking the courtyard), before dressing and running out to catch the *Metro* to work.

Walk to the supermarket for that night's dinner provisions, instead of taking the car for a big stock-up. Try choosing different food than you normally would – **imagine you live in Paris as you shop** – what would you cook for dinner if you were your ideal French girl?

Enjoy a glass of sparkling mineral water and a small dish of olives as an apéritif, rather than potato chips and a soft drink. Relax while you **enjoy your cocktail time** before dinner.

Retire to your bedroom earlier than usual for a leisurely face wash and time to read. If you have a CD player or iPod dock in your bedroom, play relaxing music softly (the type you hear in a spa or beauty therapy salon is lovely at this time). Try painting on a face-mask for while you are reading; after washing it off take the time to massage in your night cream. You won't believe how calm you feel when you are nodding off to sleep later on.

If you can manage it, **turn off your phone**/laptop/tablet before you have dinner *and don't turn it on again until the next day*. I don't do this every night, but it makes the world of difference when I do – I feel more peaceful and relaxed; I sleep better as well.

As you are walking along the street, **hum *La Vie en Rose* to yourself** and pretend you are strolling through Paris – it helps get you into the mood to be chic and look after yourself. No-one has to know, they simply think 'look how happy that woman seems' as you glide past, with a contented, serene half-smile on your lips.

Thirty Chic Days inspirational idea:

Think of ways you can make your daily tasks more enjoyable by acting as if you were your ideal, most chic self. **Change your mental backdrop to Paris** and *have fun.*

Day 2
Eat real food

I am not one of those people who naturally chooses the healthy wholefood option. Sometimes I feel like I'm a small child; when my eye catches a junk food advertisement I am instantly hungry for that item. I admit I have felt like a dieting failure in the past, when I am 'sticking' to a healthy eating plan yet can't seem to prevent the cravings that overcome me.

I've often wondered why I make things so difficult for myself. Surely it can't be that hard to choose food, feel good about it and be healthy? How have humans survived for so long if eating is this fraught with anxiety?

It all started with the industrial food revolution and the introduction of processed foods in the 1950s; our bodies have simply not evolved quickly enough to deal with the addition of physically addictive substances such as refined sugar, fat, salt and wheat into our everyday foods. These products are also heavily advertised which can fool us into thinking they are part of a normal diet.

Why we can't stop eating junk food

Do you want to know why we can binge on junky food but not on good, real food? There is actually a proper, medical reason why we can eat processed food until the cows come home, yet one or maybe two pieces of fruit will be all we desire in a sitting.

Potato chips, lollies/sweets/candy, ice-cream, soft/fizzy drinks/soda pop and fast food 'meals' have virtually no nutrition, and our body needs nutrients to survive, not just calories.

Our physical body has been perfected by nature over thousands of years; this miraculous creation guides us to continue eating until we reach the nutrition levels required, so we eat yet more junk, feel worse because we are still denying ourselves nutrients, continue getting fatter... it's not a pretty story.

Compare this with real food. Real food nourishes and satisfies you. An apple quenches your thirst, fills you up, the fibre is fabulous for your innards and it has vitamins galore. It's the same with a colourful salad made from fresh vegetables.

This is another of my food criteria I've realised. *Can I stop eating it?* It's not like once you've had a fresh, crunchy piece of celery that you *have* to have another and another and another.

It is always unchic, unhealthy food which I cannot stop eating once I've started, or cannot have in the house without it calling my name (I'm talking to you, Copper Kettle potato chips, Sea Salt flavour).

Become a food snob

Why don't you decide to become a food snob, where unstylish food would never pass your lips? Don't torture yourself by choosing to eat 'foods' that you know will make you feel unhealthy. Your physical body needs you to look after her.

Imagine you live in a divine (yet petite) Paris apartment. Would your tiny kitchen cupboards contain large colourful bags of potato chips and packets of chocolate biscuits/cookies from big-name mass market brands? (Who, by the way, do not have your health in their interest, just their profits.) *Non*!

Perhaps your cupboards might have jars of staples such as pasta and rice, a few tins of tomatoes and tuna for a last-minute dinner. Your fridge would likely not have giant-size bottles of diet cola; rather a bottle or two of sparkling mineral water and maybe a bottle of wine. You could have cooking sauces, such as oyster sauce for a quick Thai stir-fry, a few cheeses, a small selection of fresh fruits and vegetables. Doesn't that sound far more chic?

At home our kitchen is what I would consider medium-sized while others might call it small. It is still bigger than my ideal French girl's Paris kitchen though, so I try to honour it by buying as little processed food as possible. My ideal shimmery-mirage goal would be to have *nothing* in packets, just ingredients in jars.

Make small changes to your meals

I have two tips which have helped me in my goal of replacing processed foods with real foods. Making this change is the real secret to successfully (and permanently) achieving your healthy and slim lifestyle goals.

Tip no. 1: Think what you can add to meals rather than take away from them. If you are told 'you can't have this', it is forever in your mind as a forbidden treat, which only increases its desirability factor.

But if you go the other route and ask yourself 'what nutritious component can I add to this meal?', it feels better. Over time those higher-quality additions will begin to crowd out the less nutritious components.

Having three balanced meals per day is commonly acknowledged as the best way to eat, it's been this way for thousands of years. I certainly function my best when I eat breakfast, lunch and dinner.

Tip no. 2: Make tiny changes over time. Rather than give my diet the radical overhauls that had failed so spectacularly in the past, I decided to tidy up one tiny area at a time – working on a single habit that would stick before I moved onto something else.

The key was not to change everything at once; that way my taste buds became accustomed to a new way of eating and there was less chance of self-rebellion against my well-meaning plans. I inched my way into better health and a slimmer physique. Some of the small daily habits I started years ago I still do now, so making tiny tweaks definitely helps with lasting change.

An example of this might be your daily hot drinks. If you always take two sugars in your coffee, try decreasing every few weeks to one-and-a-half, then one. Soon you'll be at no sugar and you won't even mind. In fact, if you go back to two sugars, it will taste awful.

I started using a smaller cup for my soy latte in the mornings and asking for a small size when out. There was no need for me to have a bucket-sized coffee, no matter how much better the value seemed or how much I enjoyed the taste.

I also changed to buying an ice-cream from the convenience store when I had one every so often. It was far worse value, but the alternative meant buying a big box of ice-creams from the supermarket which meant they were available in my freezer at home every night.

Can you tell that one of my stumbling blocks is being thrifty? In the end I actually saved money on both these things because I was spending less, even though the item cost comparatively more.

I was slimmer, *and* I was training myself into good habits.

Breakfast

My first tiny change was to add a piece of fruit to my breakfast each morning. As a child I ate fruit most days because my mother gave it to me, but as an adult I barely ate any at all and I knew it was healthy to have fruit in your diet. It was hard to find a good piece though – too ripe or not ripe enough. Nature is far more variable than uniformly manufactured *faux* foods! Further reasons were that it went off quickly, it was expensive, I thought it was boring to eat – my list of excuses carried on and on.

I did know that fruit was a miracle food of antioxidants and vitamins, and that all the varying colours of the numerous types meant different nutritional benefits were offered. I wanted to include fruit daily, so I found an area to slot in a piece without jostling my little mind too much.

I decided that no matter what I had for breakfast (there were no rules or diets – I continued on with the same breakfasts), I'd add a piece of fruit. One of my staple breakfasts at the time was peanut butter on wholemeal toast, so I'd have a washed and sliced apple alongside that.

Another breakfast I liked if I had more time was rolled oats simmered on the stove. My favourite way to add fruit was to dice a pear and cook it with the oats.

This, along with a handful of raisins and a sprinkle of cinnamon was absolutely delicious and felt so gourmet, I didn't even need to add sugar at the table as I did with plain oats.

As time went on I found that fruit grew from being a side to the main part of my breakfast. I now love washed, chopped seasonal fruit with a dollop of good quality (unsweetened) yoghurt on top and a sprinkle of raw mixed nuts.

In the summer I'll have a breakfast bowl of watermelon, blueberries, nectarine and peach; in the winter my chopped fruit is likely to be apple, pear and banana. I chop mine fresh each morning but you could easily chop a small container the night before, so all you'd have to do is tip it into your bowl in the morning. If your day starts early you could take it to work in a Tupperware container, complete with yoghurt and topping.

I find that this breakfast, along with my milky café latte keeps me full until lunchtime. Sometimes I have my café latte not long after my fruit, and sometimes I save it until mid-morning as a filling morning tea.

Lunch

Lunch used to be a real problem area for me. I've never had any issues figuring out what to have for breakfast or dinner, but lunch stumped me. So I quizzed myself 'if I was a chic French woman in Paris, what would I have for lunch?' The answer came to me – a gourmet salad with a piece of baguette on the side.

However, salad seemed so boring and I avoided raw vegetables if I could get away with it. I enjoy all kinds of cooked vegetables – who doesn't love crunchy roast vegetables, steamed vegetables dressed in olive oil or crispy stir-fried vegetables. But salad? I just couldn't get excited by it.

I used the same strategy as for breakfast and decided I could eat whatever I wanted for lunch, serving a side salad with it. I started purchasing basic salad ingredients such as lettuce, tomato, cucumber, celery and carrots and (apart from the tomatoes), kept them in our fridge at work. This might not be suitable where you work so you could prepare a small salad the night before and take it with you.

There are many salad places around these days and, if you don't mind the cost, go for it. But I am a thrifty girl and couldn't pay as much for a prepared salad for one day, that the same amount would keep me in salad ingredients for a week from the greengrocer.

So I started my 'add salad to lunch' plan and endeavoured to have it made up before I started my lunch, because if I'd finished my bowl of soup, leftover pizza or cheese baguette and still had to wash and chop salad vegetables, well, I wouldn't have eaten salad that day. It actually looked quite chic on our lunch table at work, with my lunch 'main' and a side salad next to it. I also found that my lunch 'main' didn't need to be so big when I had a salad as well.

I love creamy dressings so I made sure to keep my

favourite dressings stocked in the fridge. Alternatively, I have a salad sprayer bought from a kitchen store – it is filled with equal quantities of extra-virgin olive oil and gourmet balsamic vinegar. This is delicious misted over my salad when I feel like a cleaner taste than the creamy dressings.

This was a new mind-set for me as well and it goes along with the moderation theme. My old way of thinking was 'I am having a salad; the creamy dressing is too high in fat and unhealthy, so I'll have my salad plain or with a dash of balsamic vinegar only' and I would stop having daily salads as soon as I finished my diet.

This way, by using dressings I like, I look forward to my salad.

As with breakfast and as time went on, the salad overtook lunch and now *is* my lunch. I don't even have the baguette slice any more. I have a big bowl of delicious salad ingredients and protein (cold roasted chicken or quartered hard-boiled eggs) plus treats such as a sprinkle of grated cheese, fresh avocado or diced leftover roast vegetables. You wouldn't believe how delicious small cubes of roast pumpkin, onion, carrots and kumara (sweet potato) are on top of your salad.

My lunch salads with leftovers are the best; even my husband now has salad every day, and you know how most men feel about salads. When he saw how nice my lunch looked when I was making it (we work together), he too came to have salad as a bigger and bigger component of his lunch until it *was* his lunch.

To finish off your chic and *très* French meal, sip a cup of coffee or tea with a square of good quality dark chocolate; you will not only feel like you have dined at a stylish French café, but also have made your body very happy.

This usually gets me through to dinner time, but in case I feel hungry around 5pm and know that I will feel weak and dizzy by the time we eat at 7pm, I have a couple of small crackers with a slice of cheese on each or a sliced apple and a handful of almonds. This usually only happens if I don't have enough protein at lunchtime.

Dinner

Dinner has always been an easy one for me. I enjoy cooking at home and love making vegetable-rich meals. I always have some kind of meat or fish for protein and don't often have grains such as pasta or rice.

I love roast meals in the oven, even in summer. I know that sounds strange, but they are such an easy meal to make. You can roast a chicken or a piece of beef or a leg of lamb which, along with all the vegetables means you have instant protein and extras for your lunch salad.

I also use our crock pot (slow-cooker) year round – not a lot – but regularly. I find that with slow-cookers most meals end up tasting 'the same' – there can be a distinctive flavour about slow-cooked food. I have tried different recipes in my slow-cooker with varying degrees of success. I thought I would use it mostly when I was at work, but interestingly enough I use it more often when I have the day off.

When I'm at home I become enthused mid-morning to have a chop-a-thon, filling our crock pot with all sorts of meat and vegetable goodness, then have a play around with herbs and spices, stirring in a can of tomatoes or whatever I find in our pantry. A dollop of sour cream or cream cheese near the end makes it extra-tasty. I then have the luxury of not having to prepare dinner later in the day because it is already cooking.

No matter what is on the menu, I always include loads of fresh vegetables. Colourful vegetables such as broccoli, green beans, cauliflower and carrots which I steam take up half the plate; then starchy vegetables which might be roasted, mashed or boiled take up a quarter of the plate and our meat portion takes up the other quarter. That's three quarters of a dinner plate filled with vegetables!

In the summer we use the barbeque regularly – we might have steak or chicken breast with steamed vegetables. It's quick to cook and the kitchen doesn't heat up too much. I love making a simple cheese sauce to go over chicken breast, and mushrooms and onions cooked on the barbeque accompany steak beautifully. Sometimes we have new baby potatoes, sometimes we don't.

You can see that by making tiny changes at each meal you can add extra real food and nutrition into your day, reducing foods that aren't as good for you. It might not happen at every meal, but each step in the right direction counts and will build into better habits (which means better health) over time.

You don't have to do a massive makeover on your diet, just start tweaking things and adding good stuff in. It's those tiny steps that start us off; they're so small we can slip them in without setting off the alarm bells in our brain that thinks we're embarking on yet another restrictive diet. Phew!

Thirty Chic Days inspirational ideas:

Give up 'kid food'. We are adults, so there is no reason to eat children's treat food. I've told myself it's time to grow up. Since it is only my husband and I, there is no need to have any juvenile food in the house at all. By the same token you do not want to eat at fast food places painted bright colours – you will not find it to be a chic dining experience!

Get out of the diet mentality by promising yourself you can eat *anything you like* as long as it is *chic* and *real*. How thrilling a premise does *chic* and *real* sound? No more dieting. It makes me think of delicious foods such as creamy camembert, crunchy red apples, a perfectly petite eye fillet steak or a frothy *café au lait*.

'Chic' also applies to the portion size, so I eat a 30g/1 oz. wedge of camembert sliced on crackers... not the whole round.

Know how to feed yourself. Read up on nutrition to understand why junky foods make you fat. Knowing how your body is unable to process certain foods effectively can be enough to put you off them. That is the key to a healthy and slender life, *wanting* to eat the foods that are best for you.

The good news is that the more you have of something, the more you want it – this applies equally to real food and junk food, so why not focus on getting more real food into your life.

Be wary of sugar. Sugar is the real culprit that's making us fat. Try going for a week without sugary foods; you will see a big difference both in what you weigh as well as how you feel.

Start with the obvious (sweets, fizzy drinks, ice-cream, potato chips, biscuits/cookies), then if you want to, move onto hidden sugars (tomato sauce, cooking sauces, even my soy milk was high in sugar).

I seem to have struck a happy medium and a way of eating I can sustain by cutting out obvious sugars and living with the rest. I don't crave sugar as much whilst still happily indulging in two squares of 70% cacao chocolate nightly.

Day 3
Bathe yourself in mystique

Something I love to practice is the art of mystique. Nothing is less attractive than someone constantly speaking or complaining about their appearance or other aspect of their life.

We all know that person who has a steady stream of consciousness coming from their mouth. Very little passes their eyesight that is not commented on and, when there's a lull, they'll bring up something inane from the past. Complaints? Yes, there are plenty. It's much easier to criticise than find good and happy topics to talk about and, let's face it, who wants to be accused of being a Pollyanna?

Do you know how I can speak with great authority on this? Because I have been that mindlessly non-stop talking and complaining person many, many times in the past, sadly I still am on occasion! It's something I have to be vigilant about; thankfully, awareness is the first step.

I have to remind myself that those around me (particularly those closest to me) *do not* need to hear every fleeting thought that passes through my head, or know that I have a bit of a headache today. My goal is to only speak if something is important or positive; like my mother always said – 'if you can't say anything nice, don't say anything at all'. It's soothing to have peace and quiet in between times.

So let's stop, take a deep breath and reset. We are chic beings; we consider how we look and sound from the outside, rather than staying stuck inside our heads with a loudspeaker on broadcasting every little thought. We need to think as if we are the other person observing us. This never fails to help me out when I'm flailing for conversation or am trying to halt my embarrassing babbling.

It's helpful to remember that we don't need to fill every gap in the conversation and that there can be beauty in companionable silence.

Accept compliments graciously

If someone compliments you on a top you are wearing, say 'thank you, I'm glad you like it' or 'thank you, I love it too'. Don't say 'oh, I've had this for ages, but it's getting a bit old now' or 'I bought it today, it was on sale'. Or even worse, 'Oh thanks, but I think it clings to my muffin-top a little bit. See? Here?'

Why bring your insecurities into the conversation? This only draws attention to parts of you that you'd rather people didn't notice: by pointing them out you are helpfully shining a spotlight on those parts. Don't feel you are misleading people if you answer their 'you look lovely today' with a simple 'thank you'. Even if you are having a fat day, that's to do with you and no-one else, and the 'fat day' may only be in your head.

This exact thing happened recently when I complimented a woman on her complexion which was soft and finely textured. 'Oh, I've been getting terrible spots lately, and at *my* age!' She even showed me where they were. Her complexion was still gorgeous (I'd been looking at her forehead and cheekbones), but now I was staring at the spots on her chin. I admit, I do this too sometimes. Why is that? Are we afraid of seeming too full of ourselves by accepting a sincerely meant compliment?

Most people don't actually perceive others' problems, the rest may even rejoice in them. How much better would it be to glide into a room confidently and serenely, making conversation with people by being interested in them and asking questions. The less you say about yourself, the more people will want to know and, be genuinely charmed by you.

Your age is no-one's business

There is no reason to talk about your age. It's not that you're trying to hide it, but it's nobody else's business

– let them wonder. Even though I try not to, sometimes if I find out a person's age, it changes the way I view them. Remember though, age is only a number and there are those who seem older than their age as well as those who are youthful for their age, both in looks and how they act. I truly believe that age is a state of mind.

What I want to be is the best me I can be right now – age doesn't even come into it. I aim to be the best version of myself, in this moment. Half the time I forget how old I am and if I need to remember I check the year and count back from there. Really!

A friend of mine whom I met a few years ago had 'an occasion birthday' (one that ends in a zero) not long after we became acquainted. I always thought it was her fiftieth; one day years later we were talking and she said no, she's actually in her sixties. She looks amazing, and I believed the younger age because she is so vivacious. She is slim, healthy and dresses in a classically elegant way; it's the simplicity of her wardrobe paired with age-appropriate updates that gives her an air of youthfulness. She definitely goes by the French girl's manifesto of dressing in classic pieces in a neutral colour palette, livened up with a touch of the latest trend.

Of course, your close friends are bound to know your age and you theirs, but for everyone else it doesn't matter. Not having an age pinned on us makes us a little bit of an enigma, and wouldn't we all like to have an air of mystery about our person?

There are not that many situations where someone will ask outright what your age is; if it's somewhere like the doctor's, of course you'd tell them. But I've seen too many women blurt out their age in a social situation along the lines of 'I'm 51, you would have thought I'd learned that by now!'

If someone is rude enough to ask out of a sense of nosiness, there are many great comebacks. Some of my favourites include – 'If I told you I'm afraid I'd have to kill you', 'On a good day I feel twenty, but on a Monday morning...', 'twenty with some years of experience', 'oh gosh, you don't want to know', '29!', or 'you go first!'

If you respond in a jokey way and friendly tone of voice following up with a subject-changing question such as 'enough about me, what's new with you?' you'll be skilfully diverting the question in no time.

Being private at home

When you are at home with your beloved and your family, create a little mystery around yourself. Close the door when you brush your teeth, don't blabber on about every little thing you're thinking of and don't ask your husband which shoes or jacket looks better. Instead choose for yourself then make an entrance into the room, accepting a compliment with pleasure.

It is sometimes easier to learn mystique from someone who doesn't have any. Do *you* want to be that person that others learn from? It's different with family and close friends, but even then you will want to keep your marriage relationship details private. It is many men's horror that their other half will blab embarrassing details to their friends or family about them.

I know of people who don't tell family members private information because they know they will be unable to keep it to themselves. Remember, it's not only that one person you are sharing with, it's whoever they might tell also. It is respectful of others to not spill their secrets, insecurities or private happenings.

A foolproof way of knowing if it's okay to relay information about a person is – would I say this if the person was standing right next to me listening to the conversation as well? Or, would I send this email if the person I'm mentioning was reading it over my shoulder? I love this test because it works every time.

Be fun and breezy to talk to

When someone asks how you are, reply 'fabulous thank you, and you?' Then start with a few questions such as 'how is work this week?', 'how was your weekend', 'do you have any holidays planned?' or 'have you been to any movies lately?' It is actually polite not to share too much or be too intense when having a friendly chat with someone.

Mystique is not being secretive, it's more that you are not boring others with unimportant, uninteresting details of your life. Mystique is also a form of self-preservation. There are unkind souls who seem to take a perverse pleasure in the bad luck of others; sadly, it might be those closest to you.

If they don't know you are five kilos over your ideal weight or that you can't seem to get motivated at the moment, they can't make 'helpful' yet cutting comments about it. Better to let them think everything is bright and breezy with you.

Actresses who don't talk about their private lives who are rarely in paparazzi photos seem to be so much more alluring and interesting than those who give interviews to gossip magazines all the time and are out courting photos as they go about their daily life. The former also seem more secure in themselves and happy with their lives outside of the celebrity industry.

I know which one I'd rather be like.

Thirty Chic Days inspirational ideas:

Aim to spend a whole day where you **channel your ideal French woman's mystique**. Don't bring others down with your aches and pains, or thoughts on a new diet. Think about what your words might sound like to others before you speak. Be positive, upbeat and happy. You'll find this will affect *you* positively as well.

Even if you are close to your other half, there is no need to explain every single little thing you are doing or thinking. If you feel like talking as I know I often do, **hum a song quietly** instead. I like 'Moon River' or 'Dream a Little Dream'. Audrey Hepburn sang Moon

River in *Breakfast at Tiffany's*, so when I sing or hum this song to myself I always feel a little more elegant and Audrey-esque.

Try **dressing up more** without announcing it. I am famous for this (the announcing part rather than the dressing up part). I love the crisp shirt look but am not big on ironing. Rather than trumpeting to my husband that I am turning over a new leaf and will wear freshly ironed shirts every day, why not do it without comment, enjoying the sense of wellbeing it brings (then accept the 'you look nice today' with a simple 'thank you' and a smile).

Day 4
Make up your eyes

When I was younger, I didn't spend much time on eye makeup, mainly because it was hard to learn, took ages and I couldn't really be bothered. There were sometimes disasters with bright or dark eyeshadows. It was much quicker to put on a bright red lipstick and a sweep of blush, then all I needed was a couple of coats of mascara.

Fast forward to 'a certain age' and I feel I can't get away with that look anymore. Red lipstick looks too harsh and it also bleeds above my mouth (you know, into those lovely little vertical lines).

In one of Bobbi Brown's beauty books she said that spending time on your eye makeup pays dividends. Eating and drinking when you're out means you won't have much lipstick left so, if you go with the red lipstick/not much eye makeup combo you will look like you haven't done anything once your lipstick has worn off. But by going for a more defined eye makeup with a nude, glossy lip combo instead, you will always look polished.

I tried this tip when we had plans for a special dinner because I often used a deeper lip colour at night but then spent a lot of time reapplying it (despairing at the dark ring it left around my mouth after eating – so attractive).

The evening of our dinner out I applied neutral coloured eyeshadows – slightly more than usual – then defined my eyes with a dark charcoal eyeliner, smudging it into the lash-line. Mascara came next, much more than I would normally use; two or three coats top and bottom, even coating the tops of my top lashes. I tidied up by dabbing around any specks of mascara on the skin with a cotton bud (Q-tip) dipped into a tiny amount of liquid foundation.

Doing this meant I needed less of everything else – minimal foundation and powder, just enough to even out my skin-tone, and a glowy pink blusher. I finished off my look with nude lip-liner all over the lips, topped with a sheer gloss.

I was so pleased with how my makeup lasted throughout the evening. When I saw myself in the bathroom I still looked fully made up, even though all my lip colour and gloss had gone. That Bobbi Brown, she knows what she's talking about.

I also do this for work now, then if I don't get a chance to touch up my lip colour I still look good.

Study your eye shape and colour

My eyes are hooded and I've always had problems with where to put the eyeshadow and eyeliner. I googled 'hooded eyes makeup' which brought up the YouTube channel of makeup artist Stephanie Lange. She has hooded eyes too and is an expert on making them up.

Just like finding a hairdresser who has the same hair type as you, it also seems sensible to search out a makeup artist with the same kind of features that you have. They will know how to best deal with them.

I learnt new techniques from her which improved the look of my eye makeup. I stopped wearing eyeliner on the bottom of my eyes as it drags the eyes down. I decluttered any shimmery eyeshadows (except for one light colour to use sparingly as a highlighter) now using only matte shades. I also received permission from Lange to keep piling on the mascara, as she said that's what hooded eyes need.

I always thought my hooded eyes were a flaw, but I've had them all my life so accepting they are a part of me feels much better than longing for them to be different. I am grateful that my eyes are healthy – someone without eyesight would *wish* that having hooded eyelids was their only problem.

Research ways to do your eye makeup to best enhance your eye shape, then practice applying it. If you need to purchase a makeup product, make the most of the opportunity by having a makeup lesson with a department store expert. Many of these ladies are trained in makeup artistry in addition to having a passion for makeup. I wouldn't like to take up their time if I'm not planning to buy anything but, when I do need something, it's the perfect time to have an expert help me out.

Watching makeup artists on YouTube is certainly an eye opener too (no pun intended). The way they dab and blend is so different from my usual slap dash approach, so I was happy to learn how to improve my techniques.

Ultimately you want to have fun learning how to make up your eyes – look upon it as an enjoyable way to enhance what you were born with. Don't be in a hurry – take your time and enjoy the process, feeling like the artist that you are. If you are terrible at it or have a makeup disaster, don't worry, it washes off and you'll get better each time you do it.

It's also telling if you don't think you have the time – are you someone who always puts everyone else first? It can feel indulgent to spend an extra ten or fifteen minutes on something that others may think is frivolous, but you have to treat yourself well before anyone else can.

You don't have to wear as much eye makeup as the beauty enthusiasts either – my makeup is still light; it suits my classic personal style and it's what I feel happiest with.

Try different mascaras and replace them regularly

I used to have quite a few mascaras on the go at once – lengthening, thickening, different colours. I'd never know how old they were though, because I rarely used one up.

It wasn't until I read how mascaras are the number one makeup product that should be replaced regularly that I threw out all my mascaras, committing to using one at a time. I didn't want to give myself an eye infection from old product so having 'only one' mascara to choose from was a small price to pay.

I don't have a favourite mascara brand because I enjoy trying different types. It's a matter of trial and error, plus the good thing about mascaras (apart from the money aspect) being replaced every three to six months is that it provides a chance to try a different one each time.

I try to make mine last six months but usually it has dried up (or been used up) before then so I purchase a new one when I notice my mascara is getting harder to use. I leave it until my mascara has almost run out before I buy a new tube because I want it to be as fresh as possible.

I once bought mascara on a special offer then put it away because I'd not long started a new one; six months later when I came to use it, it was quite dry, but by that time it was too late to do anything about it. I'd wasted money instead of saving it.

I don't like waterproof mascaras because they are difficult to fully remove (even with a specialist eye makeup remover). I feel like I'm pulling the delicate skin around my eyes too much. I prefer normal non-waterproof mascaras – my eye makeup melts away easily at night with normal cleansing lotion and a facial tissue.

Clean-up tips

My best tip for applying eye makeup is to have cotton buds (Q-tips) handy for tidying up during application. A cotton bud dipped in a tiny drop of liquid foundation is perfect for erasing mascara from where it shouldn't be. Finally, dust under your eyes with a clean blusher brush (the small brush you receive with a blusher compact) to sweep away any fallen particles of colour.

I carry the same type of small clean blusher brush in my handbag with my pressed powder and lip gloss. I use this tiny brush to gently dust under my eyes when I touch up my makeup. I'm not putting any powder there, but it cleans up those tiny dark specks you sometimes get from using eye makeup, in a much gentler way than using your fingertips.

The beautiful effect of groomed brows

Please remember your brows – they frame your face and, done well can actually make you look more youthful. I don't go to a professional brow plucker or waxer, simply tidying my own once or twice a week. It's a matter of keeping them in a neat, natural shape as well as not taking too much off.

Don’t go mad with the tweezers because sometimes the hairs won’t grow back or will grow in crooked. Quite bushy brows are in at the moment, but I don’t think there will ever be a time when natural, tidy brows are *out* of vogue.

I often use an eyebrow pencil which I use to sketch in lightly then brush up the eyebrows with an eyebrow comb or a clean mascara wand. Finding the right colour for your eyebrows is important because you don't want to look like a freak. I find blonde pencils can be a little orange for me; grey shades are better because of the ash tones in my hair. I found this out by having a cosmetic consultant try different colours on me.

My final eyebrow tip is from the late Elizabeth Taylor. I read once that she advised keeping your eyebrow pencil as sharp as a pin, so I always keep a pencil sharpener handy to refresh my eyebrow pencil often. I have also enjoyed using wind-up eyebrow pencils that never require sharpening. I wonder what Ms Taylor would’ve made of those?

Thirty Chic Days inspirational ideas:

Give yourself the time. Take fifteen minutes extra before going out, whether it’s to work or out with friends or loved ones, to make up your eyes more fully. Accept the compliments on your rested appearance graciously.

Experiment when you're having a day at home. One day when you're not going anywhere, practice making up your eyes much more heavily than you would normally. You might think it looks too much, but live with it for the day. When I've done this, I've been pleasantly surprised by my reflection in the mirror when passing by whilst the added bonus is that my husband thinks he's come home to a bombshell!

Streamline your eye makeup into a group of products you know you will use. Donate or throw out the rest and clean up what you are keeping. Polish and dust eyeshadow cases inside and out and sharpen pencils when you put your items back. Everything will seem so new – it's wonderful; you will then see if you have any gaps that you need to shop for.

Use up your shortest eye pencils first – it's satisfying to condense numbers if you have a few. It's like the debt-reduction snowball method but applied to eye pencils (you won't find this in any financial textbook though).

Use the One Mascara technique. If you have more than one mascara, keep the newest and throw out the rest. If you have one mascara that's sad and dry, what are you waiting for, go out and treat yourself to a lovely fresh tube!

Day 5

Create and guard your secret garden

A secret garden is that sacred, private place where you are free to dream about your greatest desires safe from the judgement of others. The term secret garden is sometimes used to describe the state of being discreet and not revealing everything about yourself, but it also represents a place where you enjoy being alone to recharge and refresh.

Your secret garden is where you dream of how beautiful and successful your life will be. It holds safe all those plans and thoughts that you might think others will make fun of or scoff at and tell you to 'get real' about, but you know better; dreaming of an enchanting future makes you feel happy and inspired.

Keep your secret garden secret

Some secret gardens you can see and touch – they are physical places, others are in your mind; the latter are the best ones for keeping entirely to yourself. Don't learn the hard way that others may not match your enthusiasm for a plan; this may cause you to lose your own excitement for it.

Whenever I've told someone about a secret garden thought, which I was bursting to share even though a voice inside me was saying 'what are you telling them for – *they* won't get it!'; when the words came out of my mouth, they instantly seemed less attractive, somewhat lame in fact.

I've learnt a few lessons from those experiences. Now if I want to share, I'll choose my audience carefully – not just the next person who happens to be near me – or I'll start a new journal page or Word document to capture and formulate my idea. Or, simply start doing it.

I have also found when I've shared my plans when they are still in the formulation stage that, even if the other person gives positive feedback, some of my excitement and enthusiasm leaks out along with my spoken words. It's not easy to get that feeling back either, so the plan ends up going nowhere. It's as if the plan's vital energy has been dispersed and wasted; it makes total sense when you think about it – I've let it out and now it's gone.

The best way to enjoy a secret garden and all its

scrumptiousness is to *keep it to yourself* – to start with anyway – like a delicious hug. If it comes to anything bigger that you continue on with, those closest to you are going to learn about it anyway. In the incubation stage however, it's important to nurture those embryonic, budding thoughts and ideas by keeping them private.

Physical secret gardens

Your secret garden could literally *be* a garden – I know of one lady who has a small clearing on her property surrounded by trees which she calls her 'yoga garden', where she goes to stretch, practice yoga and meditate. My aunty has a beautiful kitchen garden where she spends a lot of time tending to her fruit and vegetables, from which I know she gains not only produce she is proud of, but a sense of peace as well.

Your secret garden might be housed in a dresser drawer or a box hidden away. It could contain letters, locks of hair or other mementos from the past, which can be soothing to visit every once in a while. I have one such drawer which holds journals, oracle cards I made for myself with uplifting quotes, a few inspirational books to dip into, pretty pens and bookmarks. I love visiting this drawer and thinking of it makes me feel calm too.

I adore words, so part of my secret garden is a series of journals. A few are filled with favourite quotes and excerpts from books I've been inspired by, another is page after page of goals, plans, dreams and writing ideas. I carry this last one in my handbag which means it's always handy to browse or add to when I have a spare minute. This particular journal fills me with excitement and possibility.

When I come up with a great idea, I'm excited to get it down on the page. If I have fifteen minutes to wait somewhere I might brainstorm thirty or even fifty chapter headings for a new book I'm thinking about, or write down ten goals. Giving yourself a number to reach activates the brain in a fantastic way.

Spending time with a great book, maybe even an erotic title, belongs in one's secret garden also. Our bookshelves at home are my favourite place to be with their mix of genres and enticing inspiration – French chic, fashion and style, personal development, 'chick lit', 'chic lit', classics, vintage and large format picture books. Standing in front of the shelves and plucking out a book for a read; well, this is my happy place.

My night-time routine is another part of my secret garden. I go to our bedroom a little earlier than my husband to spend time washing my face, flipping through a pretty magazine such as 'Victoria', maybe doing a few stretches or light yoga moves on the mat I keep rolled up under our bed. Five minutes of stretches makes a huge difference to how relaxed I feel when I hop into bed, it's so much easier to drop off when I'm feeling peaceful and relaxed with loose muscles.

Going for a walk listening to an inspiring podcast with my iPod and earphones is part of my secret garden too. A family member suggested I join a walking group because he thought I might be lonely walking by myself. This could not be further from the truth, but it was kind of him to care. My walking time is a period of respite in my day when I listen to podcasts or audiobooks and also work concerns out in my head. In addition, I love that I can walk as fast or as slow as I want, depending on how I'm feeling that day.

If you're a crafter like I am, you'll know that visiting your fabric, yarn or paper stash is a secret garden moment. Taking the time to have a play, look at colour combinations and plan your next project is a delightful way to relax. Even tidying and sorting my supplies is like a mini time-out for me.

Mindful secret gardens

One of my favourite examples of a mindful secret garden is the setting of an intention. You might have created a plan for yourself that you are going to remain chic on Christmas day or another special occasion such as a family wedding. Ahead of time you decide that you won't be snacking from all the bowls of sweets and nibbles around, that you will sip your drink elegantly and that you will have only one serving at the dinner buffet. You've also decided that you won't be drawn into any arguments or family drama, as well as speaking positively and not gossiping. These thoughts make you feel calm, in control. Does anyone else need to know all this? Of course not, it's only for you.

A blog makes a great secret garden to explore your personal thoughts and there are a couple of options for keeping it private if you wish. One option is that you can write under a pen name – why not choose something fantastical to indulge your alter ego? Secondly, you can write freely if you make the blog settings private, either keeping it to yourself or sharing with a handful of like-minded online friends, who must log in to read and comment.

Another type of mindful secret garden could be learning a new skill or getting fit. Sometimes it's nice to start something without telling others first. Have you ever had the experience of getting an idea, perhaps going low-carb for a while because you realise your diet has become rather heavy and you're feeling weighed down? You might mention to a friend that you're excited about doing this to release weight, however their response is not positive – 'oh don't do that, it's so hard, you'll crave carbs – I tried it and it didn't work'. Suddenly your buoyant self has a puncture and you find it's an uphill ride to get your enthusiasm back again.

Even if you eventually include others, it is fun to at least *commence* something all by yourself. I might decide that I'm actually going to have a go at learning French, so I'll listen to CDs and maybe even think about lessons. In this moment I have excitement and momentum; it doesn't matter that I don't have a trip to France planned and don't know anyone who is French. I'd simply like to have a few French language skills; it's nice to surprise people with something they don't know about you too.

Maybe it's cooking lessons from a different culture, music theory, art history, dressmaking or another type of lesson. If you explore a side of yourself that interests you without checking in on what others think, you will be giving yourself the best possible start by honouring your own desires.

It's always nice to share interests with family and friends, and I do think that is a wonderful part of life, however others have their own particular view on the world. Sometimes it's nice to show up with a project completed, instead of laying yourself bare when an idea is still in its delicate formative stages.

Benefits of the secret garden

Having a secret garden to dream of and look forward to visiting, whether it is a place or a thought, can help you get through a tough day. Having a captivating book to dip into during your lunch hour is a perfect example.

You may find a new career or business idea by exploring your secret garden. My writing started from a desire bursting inside of me which I kept secret at first, because I felt shy of sharing what I thought others may look upon as silly.

At the same time as gaining validation from my readers – who love a lot of the same subjects I do – I've gathered the confidence to love what I love and not censor myself for those who would rather live life in a more... prosaic way. Neither is right or wrong, it's just that we're all different in the way we choose to spend our days.

Having little respites to look forward to helps you relax, both at the time of anticipating them *and* when you are enjoying them. Feeling at peace is extremely beneficial to your health; everything about your person eases and this in turn is wonderfully therapeutic for both your body and your mind.

You can dream beauty into your life too. If part of your secret garden is a creative outlet, you can create loveliness for yourself and your home with handcrafts, painting or gardening.

Taking care of your secret garden is part of your mystique, so enjoy exploring thoughts and projects without broadcasting them to everyone around you. If a topic you adore does come up, join in with your point of view or knowledgeable thoughts, and enjoy the look of surprise you may get!

Thirty Chic Days inspirational idea:

Hopefully this chapter has **sparked ideas for your own secret garden**. If something calls to you, don't brush it off, honour yourself by exploring it to see where it could lead to.

Day 6
Be your own French aunt

I was lucky enough to grow up in a loving, warm, stable and happy home environment with a mother who endeavoured to give me the best of her upbringing and shape me into an elegant lady. She didn't *quite* make it since I don't enjoy ballet or live theatre, however she gave me a love of classical music, opera, dressing simply in my own style, accessorising, good grooming, kindness, positivity and a love of reading.

All this has shaped me into the person I am today. I still have my off-days though, so I've decided now that I am an adult I need to be my own upholder. To assist with this, I channel my own French aunt.

Imagine if you had a chic French aunt who lived in Paris. She would alternate visiting your home and having you come to stay with her on vacation. Your French aunt would want only the best for you by lovingly offering you her wisdom and advice, as well as inspiring you by her example. She would tell you fabulous tales of when she was younger and you would hang off her every word.

Imagine her gently guiding you, showing you how she does things whilst offering her suggestions to you. If you had a problem, you could ask her about it to learn from her chic wisdom.

Being your own French aunt means you ask a question of *yourself* to lead by your *own* example. If you are resisting something and don't know why – perhaps it's going for a walk because the weather is inclement, or debating whether to have a healthy, nutritious lunch instead of a lazy, snacky one, why not be guided by your French aunt?

'Ask' your French aunt what to do in such circumstances and listen for the answer. Some days we don't need the motivation, we do what we need to do and we do it gladly; other days, yes, we need to call on our French aunt.

Your French aunt is not bossy or mean; she is kind and caring. She wants you to live a beautiful, happy life which is why she provides a gentle and inspiring nudge towards the best course of action.

Gather chic mentors around you

I have many people in my life whom I consider to be chic mentors. They are mostly family members and friends that I love to be around because I pick up so much from them – their way of being, how they dress, entertain or decorate their homes. I feel good when I'm around them because *they* feel good in who they are.

Other chic mentors in my life may only be acquaintances through work or simply from living in the same neighbourhood, but they still have a positive effect on me. It could be a lady of a certain age who works two doors down, whom I see regularly walking past in her beautifully understated style which makes me think 'I want to be like her when I'm older', or someone who shops with us who is friendly and open, I think of them 'how lovely, what a sunny spirit she has, she's so inspiring'.

Chic mentors really are everywhere you turn, sometimes literally, if you see someone with a striking personal style whilst at the greengrocer for instance. I love to see what stylish women have in their baskets at the grocery store too. I am inspired when I see sparkling water, fresh vegetables and fillet steak. I've found that often the shopping basket does indeed match the person.

When I used to have 'uncontrollable' snack food cravings, I would honestly sneak into the grocery store, pile my basket high with *junque*, then try lining up at the cash register without seeing anyone I knew. I didn't care *that* much at the time but it feels like it looking back. One of my worst moments was when a tall, elegant acquaintance was the next person in front of me; she didn't look behind her, so didn't see me with my basket of shame – or at least I hope she didn't.

Naturally she had chic lunch provisions for the week – cans of fish, fresh salad vegetables and cheese.

I also have virtual chic mentors in the form of online friends, as well as women who have made mentorship their business through their Web sites, blogs and Facebook pages. I keep the numbers I follow quite low as well as having regular clear-outs of bookmarks so that I limit my time in front of a screen. I also find if I have too many voices, my own thoughts become drowned out, so that's another good reason to limit online influences.

I am extremely grateful to the women who have written on their blogs so generously, both now and in the past. When I'd come across a beautifully worded blog post I would print it out, which means I now have the most wonderful collection of inspiration to keep my frequency on an elegantly refined level. I was inspired to start my own blog by these generous ladies and hope I am offering something useful in return for the joy I have gained from them.

In the same vein I also treasure my curated selection of chic inspiration books by authors such as Anne Barone, Jennifer L. Scott, Vicki Archer, Alexandra Stoddard, Debra Ollivier, Veronique Vienne, Jamie Cat Callan, Raeleen D'Agostino Mautner, Pamela Druckerman, Helena Frith Powell and Mireille Guiliano.

It's thanks to all of my many and varied chic mentors that I now have my own inner French aunt to call on.

Do your practical homework

Remember at school with such classes as cooking or music, there were both theory and practical lessons? Well it's the same here. For your theory you can learn from your French aunt by seeking inspiration from others, as well as advising yourself *as if* you were the French aunt. But how can you gain practical ways of being taught by your French aunt if you don't know anyone in real life and are stuck for inspiration?

I find watching French movies and reading books translated from the French gives me a greater window into the culture. I understand the stories are fictitious, however most French movies and books were written by a French person who is immersed in their own culture. Since my husband is not a fan of subtitles, I'll sometimes go to the theatre by myself during the day if there is a French film festival playing; I also pick up DVDs to watch at home.

For me, watching French actors and actresses fills in the gap between the written word and my mind. One such movie is *On Air* (2012), where I enjoyed the main character's chic personal style and modern, elegant, minimalist apartment.

It's the same with books translated from the French. Two that come to mind are *The Elegance of the Hedgehog* by Muriel Barbery and *Hunting and Gathering* by Anna Gavalda. Both titles have been made into movies too, so you can watch *and* read.

YouTube is a fantastic resource for viewing whole

movies or excerpts. You can also search for interviews of famous French women such as Inès de La Fressange, Audrey Tautou and Catherine Deneuve. I am always fascinated by how they come across to the audience and what they are wearing. You can find interviews where they are speaking in English, but even if the video is in French without subtitles, you can still enjoy watching how they communicate and hold themselves.

For another real-life look into the French woman's world, there are documentary series that share fascinating insights. The first episode of Rachel Hunter's *Tour of Beauty* is focused on how the French woman looks after herself, whilst an episode in the second season of Anthony Bourdain's *The Layover* is about being a non-touristy tourist in Paris. Both are available to watch on YouTube and, I think, worth your time.

Being a wine enthusiast, my husband loves watching the television series *Oz & James Big French Wine Adventure* on DVD, where the presenters travel around France interviewing French people about winemaking. There are fabulous examples of both French men and women in this series; they are entirely natural in their own home or vineyard, dressed as they normally would be, plus the scenery is absolutely gorgeous.

I've saved the most *magnifique* practical lesson for last – travelling to France. It's my dream to stay in Paris or other areas of France for a month or more – to rent an apartment, live like a local and simply enjoy daily life. Wouldn't that be the ultimate practical lesson? One day...

Be the French aunt to others

You could take the French aunt one step further by being the French aunt to any younger females in your life, whether a niece, neighbour or young lady you come across when you are out. You never know the effect you can have on someone and it only takes a kind word and a smile to leave a lasting impression. I remember older women I encountered when I was younger who left either a happy or a sour impression on me.

You might be having a busy day and jump into a queue to buy something, but it never hurts to be polite and say 'after you'. Or a sincere smile to a young girl waiting for her mother outside the changing room. When I'm working in our store, I sometimes notice younger girls (primary school age) looking at me shyly while their mother shops.

It's easy to forget about children, instead focusing only on the adults with children often being ignored. However, if you talk to the child and acknowledge them you can see they appreciate it and – sadly – may be surprised by it.

I want to be remembered by someone, even if I only meet them once, as the kind lady who spoke to them as an equal, instead of someone who scowled or dismissed them as unimportant.

Thirty Chic Days inspirational ideas:

In a situation where you are feeling lazy, unmotivated or at a loss as to how to handle something, **ask yourself 'what would my French aunt advise?'** You may be surprised at the answer that pops up.

Observe chic women in your own life to see how they carry themselves. I love meeting up with chic friends and soaking in their elegant way of being.

Do your 'homework'! See if there is a French-subtitled movie that looks good coming up at your local indie filmhouse. While you are there, absorb the elegance and panache of the other attendees. I've always found that the audience is in alignment with the movie when I go to the pictures.

Look around you for any opportunities to **be a French aunt to someone else**, whether you know them well or not.

Day 7
Honour your body with chic movement

I must be the least athletic person I know; I did the minimum sports requirement at school because it wasn't that much fun to me. It seemed like such a waste of time, especially when I could've been enjoying a good book instead! Looking back, the only sport I enjoyed was running – it was solo and I could lose myself in it.

I don't run these days – walking is my preferred exercise. It truly is the perfect form of self-care – it's free, you don't need to do it at an inconvenient time and you don't have to drive to get there (unless you want to walk in a different neighbourhood for a change of scenery). If you don't have much time, rather than skip it altogether, you can take a shorter walk than usual. There are no drawbacks to daily walking.

Over the years I've – begrudgingly – started some gym membership or other and, I admit, there have been times when I've enjoyed it. However, there were also long periods in my life when I did absolutely no exercise from week to week.

When I was focused on my gym workout routine I did gain benefits, but I resented the hours it took out of my day, not to mention the steep cost of the membership. Maybe I'll change my mind one day, but that's the way I feel currently. I know people who have been attending their gym for years who wouldn't give it up for anything and I wish them all the best.

What I've discovered is that you need to find something you enjoy doing, something you can happily see yourself participating in for the rest of your life, because gentle movement of the body is so good for you in all ways – physical, mental and spiritual.

Happily, I can see myself walking daily for the next twenty years... and beyond.

Do you need special gear for walking?

The beauty of the walk is that you can start today, right now if you want to, without going shopping for a single new thing. You can finish reading this chapter, put your pretty bookmark in place then enjoy a refreshing stroll around the block. You might want to put comfortable shoes on, but that's about it.

In saying that, there are a few items I have found invaluable which I use almost every day in the appropriate season.

Good shoes. For a proper exercise walk that lasts around an hour, I'll wear my good-quality running shoes. You can often find these on sale, and they last a long time so are worth investing in, then keeping them exclusively for walking.

For an errand walk (more on that further along in this chapter), I like to wear a pair of shoes that are comfortable and supportive, but that go better with my everyday clothing.

A sports bra. I always wear a supportive specialty sports bra for my exercise walk. These are also worth the investment, as even walking causes quite a bounce. Every bounce equals stretching of the skin, so if you love your breasts and want to keep them looking nice, go and be measured for a sports bra.

Choose a fun colour – white ones can be so boring and in my experience turn yellowy-grey quickly. When you have a brightly coloured sports bra, I don't believe it matters if you can see a strap or the colour through your tee-shirt, because they are almost outerwear (not that I'd ever wear mine by itself though).

For an errand walk, I wear my normal clothing and therefore my normal bra. Even though I recommend wearing a sports bra, I would never let the lack of one stop me from going on an errand walk.

A light-weight jacket (if you live in a rainy climate like I do). I used to carry a small fold-up umbrella with me if it looked like rain; this system worked well but I was always carrying something, no matter how small. Then, one day, I bought a fabulous jacket (from outdoor store *Kathmandu* here in New Zealand) which is black with a fine vertical self-stripe and is styled like a short trench-coat complete with a belt. I'm so happy that it looks equally as attractive with my walking outfit of a tee-shirt and leggings, or to wear to work with my normal clothes when it's raining.

My rain jacket is waterproof but not quilted at all, which means I can wear it in most temperatures; if it's colder I can wear a second top underneath. You can become quite warm walking, even in winter, so you don't want a padded jacket in temperate climates. Mine has a hood that rolls up into the collar so I don't even need to take an umbrella with me.

It makes a great windbreak on a fine but cool day; I also appreciate all the pockets to put my keys and phone into.

Sunglasses. For bright days, to protect your eyes whilst looking *très chic*, wear your biggest movie-star sunglasses and feel glamorous as you walk.

The magic of the podcast

My ideal self walks most days and, since I bought myself a tiny iPod Shuffle, I am much more consistent.

Most of you probably have a smartphone or other device that you can listen to music or podcasts on, but I've only recently found out the joy of having something to listen to.

I am happy to go for a walk for an hour if I have a sixty-minute podcast to listen to; plus, I am learning so much every single day. I borrow audio books from the library, sometimes it's non-fiction and other times I might listen to a fiction book over the course of a few weeks. I download it to my iPod then delete after I've 'read' it. I love our library!

There are tons of fantastic podcasts and interviews you can download for free from iTunes. Tonya Leigh from French Kiss Life is a great one to start with; she has such an enchanting view on the world.

Walking errands

Since I started walking errands regularly, I've never felt more like my ideal French girl. At home we are lucky enough to live near a small shopping centre, so I can walk the ten minutes it takes to get there to do my banking or buy groceries for dinner.

From work I walk to the post office or bank, or to post a letter; I could drive but where's the fun in that? Being out and about, breathing in big lungfuls of fresh air feels so good and I come back to work invigorated.

One of my favourite combination exercise/errand walks is to wear my normal clothes with comfortable walking shoes and stroll around the city which is less than half an hour's walk each way. I can have a lovely window shop, maybe purchasing a few items I need before walking back. It's like being a tourist in my own town.

If you live too far from the city, why not catch the bus or train there, then walk around? I always feel *très* European when I do this. Lost in my book or iPod on the bus, I look around periodically hardly noticing that I'm not... actually... in Paris because in my mind... I am. I love the freedom of jumping off the bus too, no expensive carparking to find.

Walking like you mean it

Some days you will feel full of energy but on other days you will have less. On low-energy days I know I'll feel better once I've been for a walk, so I take it slow and make it more of a stroll. These are the days that I am happy to go out for an hour, because I know I can take it easy, strolling along engrossed in my current audio book. I *always* feel better for having made the effort.

If I'm feeling even lower on energy or in a bit of a funk, I walk around the block. It's short but at least it's something and being outside gives me a boost.

Then, on days when my energy is higher, I like to go at a quick pace whittling my waist. I twist as I walk and can feel my waist becoming slimmer with each step! I suck in my stomach, tuck my bottom under and get into a great rhythm.

Recently I took this a step further when I realised I'd

left myself very little time before I needed to be in the shower to get ready for work; I had only half an hour rather than my usual forty-five to sixty minutes. So I trimmed my route slightly and made it matter – I power-walked arriving back in thirty-seven minutes. I was so proud of myself for not skipping my walk and I felt amazing from the blood pumping around – what a great start to the day!

Walk in the morning if possible

Ever since I heard that exercising in the morning increases your metabolism for the rest of the day, I've had more motivation to walk first thing. I also walk before breakfast, because then you are using your reserves for energy rather than your meal.

I used to walk in the afternoon but I found I couldn't do it every day because of work, I'd be tired out when I arrived home, or it may have started raining. At least if it's pouring with rain in the morning I get a second chance for an afternoon walk, however if I've left it until the afternoon, that's my chance gone. I feel energised all day after a morning walk; I love thinking of all that fat-burning going on throughout the day too.

Walking is not the only activity in the world

You may be surprised to hear that there are other enjoyable activities besides walking. I talk about walking a lot because it's my favourite exercise, yet it wouldn't take long to brainstorm a list of other activities you may consider if walking doesn't sound fun to you. Personally I love my time alone which is why walking suits me, however most people are much more social than I am.

There are dozens of organised leisure groups that can easily bring joyous movement into your life without joining a gym. You could take Ceroc or swing classes, join a social netball team or jogging group, take a yoga or Pilates class or even try belly dancing. All of these have built-in commitment and community which means you are more likely to continue with them.

Plus, if you are unattached you may meet someone nice. When I took Ceroc classes as a single girl, it was fun to dance with different men; and my husband belonged to a social netball team that had equal numbers of men and women when I met him. If I'd known there were mixed teams I may have been inspired to join a group back then.

There are also many non-exercisey ways to bring activity into your day – ironing, cleaning the bathroom and toilet, vacuum cleaning, mopping your floors, decluttering, spring cleaning, weeding the garden, mowing the lawn, walking up and down the stairs during your tea break if you work in a tall building, or walking errands in your lunch hour. Instead of meeting a friend at a café, go for a walk in the park, a swim at the beach or lake, or even a yoga class.

There are so many ways to move that there must be one that's perfect for you.

Thirty Chic Days inspirational ideas:

Come up with a list of ways in which you'll **feel good about yourself when you exercise** – try for at least ten.

Write down all the reasons **why you can't exercise daily** right now.

Look at your reasons then **cross out those which look like excuses** to you.

Write down at least **ten activities you could do**, that range from reasonably enjoyable to very enjoyable. Pick one to start today!

Day 8
Be beautifully positive

Many definitions of *chic* describe a style of dress or physical appearance while a few mention elegance and poise; I would go further, adding *lightness of being* to the master list of chic attributes.

Have you noticed that the people you enjoy spending time with and look upon with fondness are usually those who have a positive, happy outlook on life? They are pleasant to be around and you can always rely on them to have an encouraging word. With these people, you don't have to be wary of any barbed compliments or passive aggressiveness.

My chic mentors have this common thread – the people I admire are typically joyful and happy; they never seem to be sulky or moody and, when they show they are pleased to see me, it makes me feel special.

You will rarely hear such people complaining; if they

speak of someone else it is invariably complimentary. As I think through the dozen or so personal acquaintances on my chic mentors list, this is definitely the case.

If I slip into a negative or cynical way of speaking, these people gently steer me around to a more positive point of view or offer an alternative way of thinking about someone's behaviour. They don't do this to embarrass me; it's simply their natural (or trained) disposition and the way they see life.

Experiences like this have led me to incorporate these types of virtues into my own way of being to form part of my personal definition of chic. As much as possible I am cheerful, upbeat and enjoy making others feel comfortable. It's nicer for the other person, and I want to be someone they look forward to spending time with; as importantly, it *simply feels good* to be a happy person.

It feels better to look on the bright side of things than the dark, to look forward to the future with excitement rather than fear and to expect the best from others (as well as yourself) not the worst.

We may think we are simply being realistic by looking at all the ways something is *not* going to work out, but we are doing ourselves a great disservice. Our mind does not know the difference between truth or lies and it believes everything we tell it, so why would we intentionally tell ourselves something that is to our detriment?

Tell a beautiful story

Author Louise Hay says she tells herself that each decade of her life gets better and better. She is now in her eighties and said it has been true so far. Of course it has, she told herself it would be!

I always believed I had a happy, positive persona but, when I took notice of the thoughts I told myself on a daily basis, I found this wasn't the case at all – I was actually quite cynical. Now I make a real effort to catch a negative thought and replace with a better one; over time this is becoming my new normal.

An example is when I wanted to write this book. What stopped me taking my writing further were thoughts along the lines of 'who would listen to you, you don't have any training (Chic University, anyone?) and besides, the publishing industry is in meltdown'.

I replaced these unhelpful thoughts with 'I have a unique voice and I know from my statistics that several hundred people a day read my blog. They must be enjoying my take on living a simple and beautiful French-inspired life. I also receive lovely emails and comments from ladies thanking me, saying how much they enjoy my writing and how it has benefited them'.

It was in this frame of mind that I felt much more inspired to write.

Practice forgiveness on a regular basis

I've certainly had my fair share of looking back over my life, berating myself for decisions I've made, but what's the point in doing that? It can't change anything because it's in the past so the only result is that I feel bad about myself.

Sure, I may have learned a few lessons as a result of these decisions so they weren't completely pointless, but I've found a much better way to think about things. *I made particular decisions to my best ability using the knowledge I had at the time.* Of course, in hindsight, there are always other ways to look at a situation but *at that time* I did the best I could.

Another way to think about 'bad' decisions is that they have all led you to where you are right now. If you changed even one small decision years ago, your life would be completely different so you might not have the wonderful people and opportunities around you that you do now. I'd take all the bad decisions I've made in the past if I could keep what I have right now – I love my life and especially the people in it.

Forgiveness is a powerful tool. I doubt there is one person on this earth who hasn't done something they wish they'd done differently or felt aggrieved by another's actions. Holding onto resentment towards others or guilt towards yourself is corrosive. The answer? Forgiveness.

When I don't feel like someone 'deserves' forgiveness (as I'm still churning up inside) I remember the saying 'holding onto anger is like drinking poison and expecting the other person to die'. This changes my mind-set in an instant; it helps me to forgive them so I can then move on – unencumbered.

Keep your vibration high

Ever since I heard of the concept of keeping my vibration (or frequency) high – because it attracts good things and it feels better – I consciously do more of those things that increase my vibration.

Firstly, there are the **health principles** – eating nutritious food, drinking water, exercising regularly and getting enough sleep are good baselines to a high frequency.

Then there are all the little things that I love to do that help me feel positive. The goal is to feel light, uplifted and expansive rather than heavy and contracted.

I keep **a small inspirational notebook** in my everyday shoulder bag; it has quotes, notes and ideas that I have collected over time. If I am sitting in the car for five minutes, at the doctor's waiting room or on the bus, I read or add to it. Having this notebook close by helps me feel excited and grateful for my life.

I **listen to inspirational audio** all the time – in the car, out walking and in my bedroom when I'm getting ready in the morning. My favourites include Brian Tracy, Rhonda Byrne, Peter Walsh, Tonya Leigh, Denise Duffield-Thomas and Dr Norman Vincent Peale among many others. I rarely listen to commercial radio and if I do not have an audiobook on hand, I will tune into a classical music station (one that has no advertisements) to soothe and uplift me.

I have gathered **positive affirmation mantras** that I repeat to myself when needed. If I feel my nose tickle which may mean a cold is coming on, I say 'I am in perfect good health'. If I find myself stressing about how on earth I am going to be able to afford to retire one day, I say 'I always have everything I need.' Whatever the current worry is, I counter it with the opposite which never fails to calm me. The one I say the most is 'I am safe today and always' – I've used this for so long that it flows into my mind whenever I am feeling anxious.

I am forever grateful. I thank the Universe every day for my beautiful life and good health, I also say thank you for little things like a good carpark or a great table in a restaurant and when I pick up 10c off the ground. I did that recently and thanked the Universe; a few days later in exactly the same spot a $1 coin was waiting for me. I was amazed – having gratitude pays!

Tend to your garden

Our minds are like a garden; good thoughts can be likened to flowers that make us happy just by them being there. Negative thoughts that pop up all by themselves are more like weeds. If we don't tend our garden regularly looking after the flowers, weeds will eventually take over.

If we never do anything about the weeds, they will begin to seem normal to us so we end up becoming that pessimistic, negative person who subtly repels others (as I mentioned before, I used to think I was being 'realistic' thinking like this). By tending to our flower garden and pulling out the weeds, soon we will have a beautiful display that is uplifting, colourful and helps us appreciate the beauty of life.

Because I was quite a cynical person, I chose instead to surround myself with calmness, kindness and positivity. I am not perfect, however I strive to think and speak well of others and myself, be a positive influence on those around me whilst generally participating in life in an optimistic manner. The more I focus on this, the quicker I realise when I am slipping the other way and can easily shift back.

Whether we are happy, healthy, chic, slim, prosperous, stylish and loving our life – or not – is because we decided to be that way. Whatever we think, we are. I now choose to think happy thoughts which helps me to tune out the little things which used to bother me.

Since I started doing this, I have felt a lot cheerier and abler to deal with life, both the big and the small things. It is such a refreshing and calming thought that I don't have to fix everything around me. You will be relieved to know that neither do you.

Thirty Chic Days inspirational ideas:

Think before you speak – is it necessary and kind?

Stop complaining – incessant daily moans are not good for serenity and happy relationships. And if it's true that what you focus on grows... who wants to find themselves with more to complain about?

Remember that **'high maintenance' is not an attractive trait**.

Remember that **complaining and whining is not chic**.

Be your own best friend and you will never be alone. *You* are a great friend, *you* are fun company, *you* can be motivating and inspiring. As long as you have *you*, you will always have a companion. Remember to be nice to your best friend as well.

Celebrate birthdays – both your own and others – with childlike enthusiasm. Getting older is a privilege that not everyone has.

Day 9

Support your signature charity

The chic woman is equally well turned out inside and out and she has a compassionate heart. She is not so self-absorbed that she doesn't see what is going on around her; appreciating all that she has makes her want to help others where she can.

These days there are so many good causes in need of funding that it can be hard to get your head around. It could be easier to ignore all of them; you may think if you can't help *everyone*, then what use is a measly donation to one of the many thousands of charities. It seems like a drop in the bucket, so what's the point?

Consider it another way though. Why not pick the cause most important to you, taking it on as your own mission? Just as one might have a signature fragrance or personal style that people recognise as yours, so too could you have a signature charity.

Your signature charity

When I hit upon the idea to have a signature charity the idea appealed. It called to my love of simplicity and it helped me feel in control of my giving. It meant I could feel okay about turning down other solicitations because I wanted to focus on the charity I had chosen.

As harsh as it sounds, saying no to other causes actually helps me help *my* charity. I know I can't help everyone, but I can feel good about making a difference to one.

Since adopting my two rescue cats Jessica and Nina, I have also 'adopted' the shelter they came from – the *Cats in Need Trust* in Auckland – as my own.

Because I don't have an endless budget I want to focus on the cause most important to me.

Your donation needn't be huge either. That's probably what stopped me in the first place, thinking it would have to be a big amount or it wasn't worth the effort. Currently I give five dollars per week to the *Cats in Need Trust* as I have been doing for a number of years now.

I also recently added a second charity – *The Animal Sanctuary* in Matakana (for larger rescue animals such as goats, pigs, chickens and donkeys among others), donating five dollars per week by automatic payment to them as well.

For where I'm at financially, I'm happy to donate ten dollars each week – it's the price of a coffee and *macaron*.

Donating money is not the only way to help

Many years ago I adopted my first two rescue cats from the *Cats Protection League* in Christchurch. Choosing to adopt rather than purchasing from a breeder or pet store is the first way in which you can support an animal charity.

By adopting, you are helping in two ways. The charity receives the adoption fee, which often only covers their costs as they usually send their charges out into the world de-sexed, vet-checked and micro-chipped, but they also now have an empty cage to help out the next needy case.

I have donated the results of my decluttering efforts to charity stores with an animal rescue theme as well. Bags of clothing, suitcases and car-loads of household items all found their way to various charity shops and my newly streamlined home was wonderful to come back to. I also like to donate to church shops and those supporting the Salvation Army and Red Cross.

I try, where possible, to donate goods directly to those in need such as blankets and towels to the Society for the Prevention of Cruelty to Animals (SPCA), and furniture and toiletries to the Women's Refuge (they can always use anything that is necessary in setting up a home).

Here are a few other ways you can help your charity if you aren't in a position to donate money:

- Donate household items, books and magazines if they have a shop, or for fundraising sales.
- Donate time. Before we had our seven-days-a-week business I spent one Sunday morning a month working in the cat-holding area at the SPCA. I cleaned cages and fed the cats. When I first volunteered I was surprised at how small the time commitment was (four hours once a month). They told me the reason – they didn't want volunteers to burn out and that frequency obviously worked for them (I was there for more than three years).
- Sell items for your charity – we sell *Cats in Need Trust* cat calendars in our shop every Christmas.
- Volunteer for 'bucket-rattling' street collections which are usually held once a year. I did this for the SPCA one year which was such fun. I flirted with men in suits at lunchtime, shamelessly emptying their wallets into my bucket. I felt like a cheap hussy (in a good way, surely there's a good way?) and I didn't mind because it was for a cause that I support with all my heart.
- Offer your skills – accounting/book-keeping, cleaning, Web site maintenance. Ask what kind of help they need.
- Donate yarn for their volunteers to knit up into different items (depending on the charity) – blankets for pet cages, blankets, booties and hats for premature babies, items to sell for fundraising, even little tops for oil-affected penguins and mother-less lambs. It is incredibly touching to hear

about all the caring ways people help out. Or maybe you are a knitter who could do some of the knitting.

- Sell unwanted items on eBay, donating the proceeds. I did this with my juicer which I was planning to donate because I couldn't be bothered making the effort to sell it online. When I had the thought that I could serve my charity better by selling the juicer instead, I suddenly gained the motivation to photograph and list it.

  Noting it as a 'charity auction' on the listing helped the price too. The buyer paid $92 for it when the price of a new juicer was $150. I paid the auction fees myself (that was my donation) and the whole $92 was given to my charity. When the young man who bought it came to collect the juicer, he said his mother (who he was buying it for) was chuffed that 'the money was going to the cats'. So cute!

Sticking with the theme

Even though I have the *Cats in Need Trust* and *The Animal Sanctuary* as my signature charities, I still do little donations here and there to different organisations. The main thing for me is that they are all animal charities.

I made a flurry of small donations to several Christchurch cat charities last year. There are still many homeless animals after the two big earthquakes in 2010 and 2011 which makes me feel so sad. I was crying as I was making the online donations. I wanted to give away $50 and thought I'd do it to five separate charities of $10 each rather than one donation of $50. Again, it doesn't seem much but it was what I had to give and I'm sure it helped a little bit. It's a much nicer way to impulse spend than going to the mall.

Online donation Web sites make giving so easy these days. In New Zealand we have *givealittle.co.nz*, run by a big corporation who guarantees one hundred per cent of your donation is given to the charity you choose. I'm sure there are similar services in most countries – be sure to check that administration fees aren't deducted, otherwise it may be better to go straight to that organisation's Web site, or donate in person.

While I am the animal charity girl, my husband is all about the returned servicemen. We have both decided that when we die, part of our estate will go to one or more animal charities, and part will go to the New Zealand RSA (Returned Servicemen's Association).

Plus, it feels good to help. An unexpected side effect of helping others is that you feel gratitude for your own comfortable and happy life; feeling grateful for all we have is a very chic way to live.

Thirty Chic Days inspirational ideas:

Research charities in your area that are most aligned with your values. There are many types to choose from such as children's hospitals, hospices, animal charities, learning disability, returned servicemen, elderly companionship and many more.

Once you have chosen a cause, read up on their Web site to **find out ways to help**. Online searches for 'ways to help X' also bring up great ideas you may never have considered.

Day 10
Simplify your life for abundance

Have you noticed that decluttering has taken the world by storm? I don't know if this term existed in our grandparents' day or if our collective habit of treating shopping as a leisure activity has necessitated its invention.

Once upon a time we shopped because we needed something and stores were open 'business hours' from Monday to Friday. When I grew up there was one late shopping night, then Saturday morning shopping was introduced; now you can shop seven days a week, twenty-four hours a day.

In addition, many goods have never been cheaper so it is easy to buy more than we could ever use. We can literally purchase anything we want, via a quick car ride or the click of a button. Couple this with clever marketing techniques that entice us to buy, whether it's on a Web site or in a bricks and mortar store, and it should come as no surprise that our homes are stuffed full of purchases that we barely remember making.

Opening up your space for more

If you have ever decluttered a room, cupboard or even a drawer in your home you will know the amazing feeling that results. It's so glorious that you have to go back to gaze around and soak in the peaceful, soothing energy.

Knowing how good it feels to have a room feel so spacious and free inspires my goal to have our whole house feeling this way, but it's not easy to achieve. There are many factors stopping me from completing my whole house decluttering project and you may relate to some of them:

I paid a lot of money for this
It was a gift from someone I love
I inherited this from someone who is no longer with us
It's still in good usable order
I might use it at some time in the future
What if I get rid of it and then need it?

To live your best and happiest life means working through all of these 'reasons' why you need to keep something. Organising expert Peter Walsh has a great way of looking at inheritance mementos you feel guilty about wanting to donate – he says that the item cannot replace the person. I watched him on an *Oprah* episode emphatically explain to a lady 'that clock is not your grandmother'. Simply put, you don't need to keep an item to have wonderful memories of the person who has passed.

When I've finally admitted to myself that I don't want to keep something and worked out whether I am going to sell or donate it, I feel like a weight has been lifted and I do feel lighter. As hard as it is to get rid of something and deal with the associated feelings, it's harder to live in a house full of clutter.

Use an outbox

A useful tool that may help you in your quest to pare down your belongings to 'only that which is beautiful or useful' (William Morris) is to have an area in your home to use as an 'outbox'. An outbox is like a cooling off area where you can place items you no longer want. They aren't gone straight away so the fear of getting rid of something you might later need is lessened dramatically.

You might think that an outbox is simply a means of procrastination that leads to nothing ever leaving the house but I have found the opposite to be true. I can be more ruthless in my decluttering, whether it's the closet, kitchen cupboards or towels and sheets, then, when I go back to look through the outbox a week later, I am happy to take everything off to be donated because none of it appeals to me anymore. It's almost as if this step breaks an energetic cord.

An outbox doesn't literally have to be a box; sometimes it *is* a cardboard box which I fill and donate, other times it might only be a shopping bag. I use our guest bedroom as an outbox too by placing items on the bed in a neat pile. We don't often have people to stay overnight so it's a great spot to place items I don't know what to do with. Within a week or two, I'm ready to drop them off at my favourite charity store.

Deciding whether to sell or donate

I can understand people wanting to sell items online in order to recoup part of their initial outlay. I have sold a few of my decluttering efforts online, however I am more likely to donate these days. The thought of photographing, writing a description, uploading, running the auction, dealing with the buyer and posting the item out seems like too much effort to me.

Unless it is a high value item, I'd rather donate it to charity. We don't receive tax deductions here in New Zealand but in countries such as the United States I understand there are tax breaks offered for donated items.

Deciding to donate rather than sell may help you make a different decision next time you are tempted to buy something you don't need. Thinking to yourself 'I can sell this online if I don't want it' could tempt you to make yet another impulse purchase, but thinking 'I could give this away when I'm bored with it' may stop you getting out your wallet.

Rethinking stockpiling

As there are only two of us in our household and we eat a mainly fresh diet, we don't get through many pantry items so I try to keep packaged foods to a minimum.

I have been caught out stocking up on food items when they're on special. I used to love the feeling of a kitchen well-stocked with food, but these days I get more of a thrill from seeing that our pantry and fridge has a high turnover of food because we regularly use up what we have. It is a much better feeling to replace something that is finished versus the feeling of begrudgingly using up a stockpile that is getting close to its use-by date, or worse, throwing out food that is too old to eat.

I may spend a little more if I want to replace a grocery item which is not on sale that week, but I know I have already saved myself a lot more by not stockpiling items that I'm only guessing we will want to use in the future.

I still remember the saga of the breakfast cereal – Weetbix – that my husband ate every morning, which I bought half-a-dozen large boxes of when it was on a super-special. He gasped when he saw all the boxes and reminded me of the small portion he ate each morning (two Weetbix biscuits).

About half way through the boxes his personal trainer changed his diet so that he ate *one* Weetbix per day. It took quite some time and a bit of ingenuity (Weetbix dessert crumble, Weetbix slice, Weetbix crumbled in a meatloaf instead of breadcrumbs) to get through all those cereal boxes.

That example still comes to mind when I am tempted to stockpile.

Feel abundant with less

I admit that I have a hard time consistently keeping my surroundings simplified and clutter-free; clutter seems to be attracted to me – I must be a 'sticky' person. I've heard of people described as 'clutter magnets' and I suspect I might be one.

It's not as if you can declutter once and be done with it either, there will always be a constant flow in and out of life – items come in so items must go out. Sometimes the balance gets out of kilter though and that is when clutter (and stress) builds up.

It's a strange irony that with less you feel like you have more, and everything you keep feels newer and more attractive to you. You might think a closet stuffed with loads of clothes feels more abundant than a minimal wardrobe but I have found the opposite is true.

When I ruthlessly sorted through my closet taking everything out then putting back only my favourite pieces, I saw how nice it looked and realised how inspired I was to dress up – my wardrobe looked like a stylish boutique. Everything that was left on my bed was placed in the outbox to 'cool off' and after a few weeks I was ready to let the items be donated.

Every so often I empty my entire large bookshelf; I then clean the shelves, go through my stacks and reorganise the books I've decided to keep. Because I've already done my big book declutter, each time I do this now only a handful of books leave. Having decluttered and reorganised the remaining titles I've found they look fresher and more appealing to me afterwards, on different shelves and with different shelf-mates than they had before.

If I know I have too many books but don't want to part with any of them I play little games with myself, saying 'I must choose twelve books to donate' and it works, I have a neat stack of twelve to drop off when I've finished. When I do things like this I instantly know which titles I want to release.

When I last did a declutter and deep clean of my kitchen, I went from having kitchen counters displaying 'useful' items such as vitamins, a container of cat biscuits and salt and pepper grinders, to storing all those items in the pantry. They were still conveniently close but I didn't need to look at them all day – cat biscuits and vitamins are not ornaments.

I also went through my kitchen cupboards taking everything out – plates, cups, glasses, pots, gadgets – everything. I then wiped down the shelves and drawers putting back only the items we used on a regular basis. I turned a critical eye to the rest and much of it was donated.

Gadgets are the hardest because they look like you'd use them, when in reality they are white elephants that you've spent good money on. I felt such freedom – and abundance – in letting all those things go and it's now a pleasure to work in our kitchen. Making meals the first few days while the novelty was still there felt like a breeze, whereas before it was getting to be a chore.

When you see living rooms that have been staged in a magazine or real estate advertisement, they always look so appealing because they only have the necessary items in them – sofas and/or chairs, a coffee table and side tables, a lamp or two and maybe an area rug. You won't see piles of old magazines, half-done craft projects, sliding stacks of DVDs or abandoned shoes that didn't quite make it to the closet.

Imagining how calm and peaceful I would feel if I lived in one of those sparsely staged homes helps me when I need motivation to streamline my belongings. It might not be easy, but it's so worth it.

Thirty Chic Days inspirational ideas:

List five areas in your home that bother you the most – it could be an area that always seems to be messy, your least favorite room, your closet or somewhere else that causes you stress.

Pick one that you know you will follow through on and **tackle it straight away**. If there are items you don't want there be honest with yourself, deciding if they will be useful somewhere else or if they need to go straight into your outbox for donation or sale.

Clean this area before you put back what you are keeping. Admire and repeat with the next area on your list. Make a plan for when that will happen – one area a week? A weekend blitz?

I promise you, starting this will change your life.

Day 11
Adopt a low-drama way of being

There is no surer way to ruin your peace of mind than with the habit of getting upset over every little thing that bothers you. How do I know this? I used to be the Queen of becoming upset or annoyed with certain people or difficult situations. My antennae were so finely tuned that I'd feel affronted at the slightest little thing and I believed that it was my right for life to be perfect. Controlling everything was exhausting!

Of course we might love for our life to be this wonderful fairytale, but the simple truth is that sometimes it isn't; in fact, you can count on things happening most days that you'd rather did not. Part of life is dealing with crises, both big and small, and it's how you handle them that shows the real you. Your flight is cancelled or you miss an appointment. You get a speeding fine even though you are constantly checking the speedometer to stay within the limit. Your husband may even leave you (my first one did).

It could be the tiniest of things which sets us off too – the other day I had a piece of paper with financial information on it which I wanted to throw away. I couldn't be bothered shredding it (because obviously it's so much effort to lean across and plug in the shredder) so I was sitting on my chair tearing it up into tiny little pieces to put in the trash. I walked over to the waste paper bin to throw it in and I missed – all my carefully torn confetti sprinkled over the floor. My husband was talking to me at the time so he watched the whole thing happen; he burst out laughing and I did too – what else could I do? – then picked up every little piece.

Sometimes these things can make you incensed, or, you can choose to see the funny side of life. It certainly feels much better.

It might be a disagreement or discussion you're having with someone. In these types of situations, I felt I was entitled to show 'how hard done by' I was, so I'd stick up for myself trying to force a situation in my favour, with no give or take.

It wasn't until I made the choice to change my way of being to that of someone who was calm and accepting that things began to change. I chose to honour my sanity by taking everything in my stride and softening my focus so I saw more of the big picture and less of the details.

When I changed so that I wasn't getting myself all

churned up over daily blips, my calm demeanour flowed through to other areas of my life and it has now become my default way of being most of the time. This is not only nicer for you and those around you but it's much better for your health – most importantly your blood pressure and also in being slimmer.

Raised cortisol levels are caused by stress whether it's perceived or real; the stress hormone cortisol contributes to an accumulation of stomach fat. By being more relaxed about things, you could help yourself be slimmer around the torso (and I don't know about you, but my torso is the first place I put on weight).

You might respond 'easier said than done, Fiona' when I say breezily 'oh don't worry about it, take things in your stride, it'll all work out', and it's still something I have to work on too. The great news though, is that every situation you come across is an opportunity to practice and strengthen your skills.

Pick your battles

You may have heard the saying 'will this matter in ten years' time?' It's such a wise question to ask and helps me not be so sensitive about things people say and, for the most part, let their words pass by without affecting me.

I tell myself 'they might be having a bad day' or 'they could have just had upsetting news' and both of these things may well be true. Or maybe they were momentarily thoughtless, regretting what they've said without me jumping all over them. It helps to remember the truth that it's more often about their stuff than it is about me.

I also don't want to give my power away by letting someone else dictate how I feel, which is helpful to remember as well. I used to know someone who was passive-aggressive in the extreme and he triggered me terribly; even thinking of him wound me up!

What saved me with this person was the realisation that I didn't want to give my power to him, that he was 'winning' if I let myself feel agitated; that thought alone meant I was choosing how to feel. *I didn't need to let him get to me*. It was, and still is, so freeing. He's going to behave exactly as he does; I can't change that and nor do I want to. I can, however, choose how I respond. After that he bothered me far less and it diminished over time, since I had already lessened the charge around him.

Picking your battles can also relate to small injustices. For example, when I'm out with friends, I go with the flow. I don't want to be that difficult person where nothing is ever good enough. Maybe because I work in retail, I notice bad or indifferent service. It used to stress me out but it was not worth the aggravation and it made for an unhappy time. Now I focus on what's fabulous about where we are.

Choosing to live this way helps not only your health but your looks as well. Being uptight and anxious is not good for you and it causes wrinkles. You know when you're annoyed by something, you can feel your face stiffening? When I realise that and intentionally relax myself, I sense all the tension dissolving. How many times do we tighten our faces unconsciously? Do all those little frowns add up to a wrinkle? I don't want unnecessary wrinkles and I'm sure you don't either.

A great piece of advice I heard for when you're feeling irate is to let your arms hang by your sides, with your hands open and relaxed, fingers dangling. Apparently you cannot be angry when your hands are like this. When you are feeling irritated, subconsciously you want to scrunch your hands up into fists, but if you don't do that, the displeasure is hard to keep.

I've tried it and it works well. Why? Because our physical state changes our mental state. Smiling when you're not happy does the same thing – amazingly it starts making you feel happier!

What would an iconic chic woman do?

Think about ladies whom we might regard as iconically chic – Audrey Hepburn, Grace Kelly, Marilyn Monroe, Greta Garbo, Katharine Hepburn and Coco Chanel. Modern examples who come to mind are Aerin Lauder, Natalie Portman, Audrey Tautou, Catherine the Duchess of Cambridge, Inès de La Fressange, Anne Hathaway, Keira Knightley, Mary the Crown Princess of Denmark and Marion Cotillard.

Can you imagine any of them having a hissy fit, being rude to someone serving them or being snippy with a salesperson? Now I'm sure none of these ladies is a doormat and that each is self-assured in her own way, but I also imagine that they take things in their stride, by letting their feelings be known in a cool and collected way.

Of course I've never met any of these women so I cannot determine if this is correct, but the poised image they portray inspires me to be my most elegantly composed self.

Imagine channelling that chicly iconic woman and not letting yourself down by being nasty, nit-picky or a drama queen.

We can't hide our true selves. How you are in your private time is most likely how you come across when you're in public. Being awful, bitchy and gossipy in private will eventually seep out into who you are publicly. It's hard work being two people so why even bother? By cultivating a no-complaining, no-upset way of life, you will be happier on the inside which always shows up as being happier on the outside.

Consider that there might be a reason for things not working out

When something doesn't go your way, instead of grumping about it and losing your cool, think about it from this angle – you are being held back because there is something even better to come. How much better does that feel?

I often think this to myself when I seem to hit every

red light on the way to work '*Oh well, there must be something up ahead that I'm avoiding being involved in. Thank you Universe*'. Whether this is true or not, it feels much better than becoming more and more peeved with each intersection.

When my first husband left me at the age of twenty-nine, I felt like my whole life had fallen apart. It wasn't a nice feeling at all and I truly felt adrift from how I thought my future was going to turn out.

Because I'd already been doing a bit of spiritual reading and personal development work on myself, mixed in amongst the grief was a tingling (and terrifying) excitement of not being in control and simply following my intuition to see what the Universe had planned for me.

What I felt inside was that I needed to move to the big city, away from the small village where I'd grown up, so I did that and created a new life for myself. Three years later, I met the love of my life there. I didn't mind waiting three years for all the happiness I now have, and I had a lot of fun in that time too. I'm still having fun in fact, married to a man who is far better for me, I just didn't know it when I was married to my first husband.

You never know what's out there waiting for you and excitingly, it's likely to be better than you could ever have imagined. Be open to change, embrace it, because it's going to happen whether you want it to or not.

Gain inspiration from the opposite angle

My lovely maternal grandmother, may she rest in peace, had so many chic qualities and in many ways was a chic mentor to me, however she was affectionately famous in our family for being a *complete drama queen.*

If one of her grandchildren broke or spilled something in her elegantly furnished flat, she'd cry 'oh no' in a deep, mournful slow voice as if a monumental tragedy had occurred.

Phone calls would be hung up on if she didn't like the way the conversation was going, she gave a good door slam and, on the odd occasion if you really ticked her off, she would simply hop in her Mini and drive away without saying goodbye.

To me these are funny stories and just part of who she was, but my mother (who grew up with this behaviour) once told me that because of this she made the decision never to be dramatic; as a result, my mother is one of the most easy-going, cruisy, happy, even-keeled people you'd ever meet. I know it has served her well.

Perhaps you know someone who is overly dramatic or complains a lot. It sounds a bit mean but could you use them as encouragement on how *not* to be? To balance out the karma, thank that person in your head for the inspiration and wish them well.

Thirty Chic Days inspirational ideas:

Choose a chic mentor to keep in mind when you need extra backup to remain composed when a situation arises. Channel her and be your higher self. Look upon each circumstance as an opportunity to practice your calm being.

Trust that the Universe has your back and try not to feel too rigid. If you don't take directions when they are offered sometimes the Universe will show you the correct way against your will, which is a lot more jarring. Go with the flow, trust in the future and you will enjoy the journey more.

Day 12
Curate your wardrobe like it is your own bijou boutique

Imagine you are strolling along a main shopping street in Paris taking in the inspiration and feeling of such a beautiful city, when you turn off into a charming little side street. There are boutiques on both sides and you step into one... there are not that many garments in the store, however you can quickly see they are each a perfect specimen of their type.

There are dark charcoal peacoats hanging on one wall, in the middle of the store a small stack of indigo denim jeans is folded neatly on an aged oak table and, near the window, the prettiest floral sundress clothes a mannequin.

Cream-coloured shelving on the opposite wall holds neatly folded stacks of beautifully cut white, black, navy and grey tee-shirts.

The boutique is filled with light; in the back corner sits a large potted palm, a huge dark-red Persian rug sits on the floor and Carla Bruni music plays softly in the background.

Such a scene is the inspiration for my wardrobe at home. Each morning when I get dressed, I want it to be like I am shopping in my own little stylish boutique.

This thought makes me happy to leave 'good enough' clothing in a store – 'good enough' is not perfect and that's what my chic boutique deserves. This dream also encourages me to pass along items which I have already bought – or perhaps been given – which I instinctively know aren't quite me.

In my mind the perfectly dressed me has a petite, curated wardrobe of items from which to choose in an effortless and pleasurable way.

What would your idealistic French girl wear?

Take some time to imagine what your dream self might wear on a day-to-day basis. Forget about practicalities such as your routine tasks, budget and what you already own. Those details can be sorted out later, but for now, let yourself dream.

Start from the beginning and picture what your most idealised and chicest self would wear. Take inspiration from your favourite celebrities, movie stars and fashion icons and also from people you know whose style you love.

For me, evocative images that come to mind are:

- Black slim-fitting capri pants with a fitted boat-neck top and ballet flats *a la* Audrey Hepburn
- Rolled up straight-leg jeans with a white cotton shirt and bare feet like Carolyn Bessette-Kennedy wore when boating with JFK Jr.
- A below-the-knee pencil skirt with a dark silky blouse tucked in and stiletto heels
- A feminine camisole top worn with sexy skinny jeans, ballet flats or pumps and a nipped-waist blazer
- Lounging at home in sexy leggings and a fitted top with my darling

Now I can think:

- What do I already have in my wardrobe that I can put these outfits together with?
- What items do I not have but would love to incorporate with other items I already own?

Then, list those items on a clothing wish-list. For the first image, I have black ballet flats and three striped boat-neck tops, but I would love the capri pants – I would wear them often as well as feel great in them (despite having a different figure and different colouring than Audrey). They would also work with my lifestyle and budget and could become a good staple in my wardrobe.

This little exercise helps me add new options to try that are in alignment with my personal preferences instead of only being led by the current fashions. Both are useful actually – I like to see what's new and what I can incorporate into my style *and* I love to keep my baseline classics.

When shopping or if I'm sorting through my wardrobe to have a clean-out, I keep a small list of words in mind. These are words that I want to describe my personal style, words that I want others to think of as they interact with me. Words such as 'sophisticated, clean, chic, stylish and simple' keep me away from the slightly frumpy items which I can veer towards easily (because I love comfort so much). With these words in mind I know instantly when an item fits that criteria and when it doesn't.

I decided that 'sexy and sophisticated' were my essence words for underwear, sleepwear and home loungewear. I decluttered items that did not make me feel sexy and sophisticated and repeated those words as a kind of mantra when I was shopping for new items. At home typing this in my loungewear of navy leggings and a navy deep-vee fine-knit merino top I do feel, yes, sexy and sophisticated. It works!

When I have a closet that contains only items that pass my essence words test, it's a pleasure to gaze into my wardrobe or drawers and see how lovely it all looks. *Très 'boutiquey'*!

Play in your closet often

To keep your wardrobe alive and prevent it from becoming stale, be sure to edit it regularly. When I do this I always gain a greater appreciation for the clothing I own.

Removing the pieces that don't fully reflect your spirit means the items remaining can shine. If you feel overwhelmed by the task, start small by sorting specific areas.

Say you start with tee-shirts: take everything out of the drawer, choosing only your favourites and newests to put back. You will find that some of your previous favourites and newests are now not so pristine, they may even look a little tired when looked at with a critical eye. It goes without saying that clothing with unmoveable stains or small holes go into the rag bin.

Tee-shirts that are still in good order but not good enough for 'out' can be your home clothes if you love them. I often downgrade like that; it means you can look attractive around the house too. Please do not be tempted to wear the tops with holes and stains at home because no-one can see you; you deserve to feel pretty all of the time.

Dust out the drawer you have emptied. If you have pretty paper (either scented drawer liners or nice thick wrapping paper, even attractive calendar pages are great), cut a piece and line the base of your drawer. Put the drawer back in then refill it with your edited, neatly folded items. Do check them as you go for any needed repairs.

Note with delight how the drawer is now only semi-full whereas before you struggled to close it. Air can circulate which is better for your clothes and you will also get a thrill next time you open that drawer because you love everything in there.

Bag up your pile of donations to distribute and put the rags in your cleaning supplies cupboard if you will use them.

Carry on through the rest of your wardrobe, whittling down as you go. I did my footwear recently; it's wonderful now to open the wardrobe door to see neat rows of shoes that I actually wear, as opposed to the big messy pile I used to have. Sometimes I sell discards online if it's worth my while, I also have a friend who is the same size as me and she happily takes them off my hands. Donating to a charity shop is the third option and, of course, worn out shoes go straight in the bin.

It can require big deep breaths to prune your wardrobe to a core of interchangeable, wearable items which all look great on you but it's so worth doing the exercise. I have gone from a wardrobe full of items which added minor stress to each day to a smaller quantity of items that I love to get dressed in.

Create your own fashion uniform

Have you ever noticed that despite advising us to wear the latest looks and colours each season, leading fashion designers and editors almost always stick to the same look?

Think about Donna Karan in unstructured black knits, Giorgio Armani in his dark trousers and navy or black tee-shirt, Ralph Lauren in jeans and a denim shirt and Karl Lagerfeld in his white high-collar shirt, black suit and crucifix jewellery. Carine Roitfeld has her staple look as do Emmanuelle Alt and Anna Wintour.

Even celebrities do the same thing. I admire Jennifer Aniston's casual style – fitted jeans, a pretty top, big looped scarf and a tailored blazer – and started collecting Internet photos of her for inspiration. I found there was definitely a pattern there.

In my own wardrobe I realised my favourite outfits – the ones I felt sexy and confident in – were all variations on a theme; they were proportions that felt right for me and flattered my figure type. Yes, I'm all for trying new things, however when I strayed too far from my ideal look I had some real fashion disasters; in one particular outfit where I felt like being a little daring and *avant-garde* (for me), I tugged and fiddled at my clothing all day yet still felt like a mess.

True elegance is when you can put something on in the morning then go through your day without giving your outfit a second thought. When you've taken the time to figure out what makes you feel and look your best and have those items in your wardrobe, then you can dress with ease every day.

The seasonal switch boutique-style

One idea I've had fun with which has helped me hone my personal style is a new take on the summer/winter clothing switch.

My new idea was sparked by the thought of cultivating my own chic boutique-style closet. If you think about a fashion boutique they rarely have items folded; instead they are mostly on hangers. As the stock won't be there long it's unlikely the hangers will make a bump mark in the shoulders of garments and it's the same with your current season wardrobe.

There are some items such as tee-shirts and knit tops which I've previously always folded and never hung, but I decided to hang everything for the current season in my closet and store off-season folded clothes in my drawers (with off-season hanging clothes in a less accessible part of my closet).

This makes such a difference when I'm getting dressed now. In the winter, merino knit tops that I might have had folded in a drawer are now hung up with my jeans and trousers so I can see all my options in an instant, making it easier to get dressed.

My off-season wardrobe is folded and clean in my drawers. When it comes to the next season I put everything (clean) from the outgoing season into my drawers and hang up my 'new' season wardrobe. Having current season items all hung together helps me weed out what I don't want because it's right there in front of me, whereas in drawers it's easy to let items languish at the back.

I use this system only for clothing that is seen publicly; other clothing such as underwear, loungewear, sleepwear and exercise clothing have their own drawers and always stay there.

Inspire yourself

My dream, and I know I will have it one day, is a walk-in wardrobe. I don't want tons of clothing though. My desire is to have a small capsule wardrobe of perfect pieces curated over time which is spaced out on hangers (or folded in drawers) so that my boutique ideal becomes a reality.

Whenever I come across a magazine advertisement for a built-in designer wardrobe I pause to admire the sparsity. Of course they only show a dozen hanging items and three pairs of shoes, but to me that's what makes it so attractive.

Thirty Chic Days inspirational ideas:

Think about **the image you wish to portray** in the different areas of your life. What five words would you ideally like to describe your personal clothing style overall? If you're stuck, think of others personal style whom you admire and come up with words to describe *their* style. You can then see what you gravitate towards.

Use these **descriptive words to help** when decluttering your wardrobe and shopping for new items.

Remember favourable comments (or the opposite) about different garments and let that guide you. If you always receive compliments on a certain outfit or even a certain colour, you can be sure it's a good one for you. **What colours or shapes do you always feel great in?**

Have a look in your wardrobe and **note down your favourite outfits**. See if there is a recurring theme in the silhouettes, pieces and colours you've chosen.

Look for pictures in magazines or online, either fashion shoots or celebrities going about their day to **get ideas on what appeals to you**. Collect these pictures, noting similarities that start cropping up. Pinterest is a free, fun and easy way to gather images.

Day 13
Indulge in your femininity

I've observed that chic women seem to enjoy their femininity, even those with a more edgy personal style. They revel in being female and enjoy playing up the differences between the two sexes, exuding elegance and feminine sophistication.

Why is it that we're so afraid of showing off our feminine side, often dressing in dowdy shapes and dark or boring colours? I am totally guilty of this. On a busy day it's all too easy to forgo makeup and scrape my hair back into a ponytail or messy bun.

Being feminine is not something to be saved for special occasions. There is so much to be gained by remembering our gentleness and softness; to celebrate daily that we were born female.

It's not only the French that do femininity well either. I can think of many examples from other cultures to inspire us – the Japanese woman with her quiet yet strong demeanour, South American women who are sensual in bright colours and their unabashed womanity, and the English lady – elegant and demure. I am of course generalising, but I do gain inspiration from all of these ladies and it's fun to channel an ideal for the day, or at least call upon one of them to extricate me from an unladylike funk.

Being feminine in the way you look

When I realise I'm being entirely too functional in the way I dress it's because I've veered on the side of masculine plainness. I've forgotten the finishing touches of accessories and am not intentionally choosing feminine styles and colours. I do try to keep on the elegant side of things but sometimes I realise I've imperceptibly journeyed across that line and need to re-remember that I am indeed a feminine being.

I'm definitely a practical person; for me, I wouldn't drift around in long, floaty floral boho-style garments, but there are many ways you can dress in a down-to-earth manner yet still have femininity.

I like to keep the lines and details of my outfits simple but there are differences in how men's and women's clothing is cut. You realise the difference when you try on a man's tee-shirt and see how boxy and unflattering it is on the female form; even something as simple as a white tee-shirt looks so much better when cut specifically for a woman's figure.

In the winter I feel feminine by wearing different coloured and textured scarves to both keep warm and accessorise my outfits. Some of my scarves are neutrals but I also have pretty colours such as a soft peony pink which adds a rosy glow to my cheeks. During warmer months, a light-weight cotton or silk scarf tied simply around my neck feels classically chic.

I decided years ago that summer shorts were not for me. Mid-thigh length did not make my legs look good and knee-length felt dowdy. I replaced these with a few summer skirts which I wear with a well-cut tee-shirt and sandals or flip-flops. I adore dresses in summer as well. Scarves are often too warm around my neck when it's really hot, so I use them on my ponytail or bun, or tied around the handle of my handbag.

Pearl stud earrings always feel pretty as well as being easy to wear; I have a pair of cultured pearl stud earrings that my nana gave me on my fourteenth birthday – more than thirty years later I still love wearing them. I alternate these with my other favourite stud earrings – a pair of simple cubic zirconias in half-carat size. As much as I admire hoops and decorative dangly earrings on other women, I feel most at home with the simplicity of my 'diamond' and pearl stud options.

Nice hair and makeup also help a simple outfit look more feminine. You don't have to go all out with full makeup and blow-dried hair; a sweep of sheer makeup and a high ponytail or a half-up hairstyle looks pretty, even if you're only at home for the day.

Feminine underwear and sleepwear

Sleepwear is a fun place to be totally feminine. Recently, when I realised I didn't have any nice winter pyjamas I treated myself to a shopping trip specifically to buy a new set. There were so many examples of frumpy pyjamas and nightdresses that I decided I would not even look at something unless it was 'sexy and sophisticated', the two essence words I'd chosen to help with underwear and sleepwear selection (as mentioned in '*Day 12. Curate your wardrobe like it is your own bijou boutique*').

Using these two words as a credo helped me easily choose a lovely pair of man-style pyjamas in taupe and cream baroque-print satin. I adore the luxurious feeling of lounging in them of a morning with my cup of tea.

I know 'man-style' doesn't sound particularly feminine but to me this style evokes old Hollywood glamour, of ladies reclining in their silk pyjamas with bobbed hair and Clara Bow lips (cigarette in holder optional).

With underwear I cleaned out any items that I couldn't imagine myself wearing as the chic Parisian woman of my dreams. Out went the smooth nude bras and plain cotton knickers. I wasn't being too wasteful as I was due for new items anyway, and it was so much fun shopping for replacements.

I have heard that French women aren't afraid for their bras to be slightly seen; for example, they'd think it was fine for lacy bra fabric to show subtly through a blouse. The rationale is that they are happy being women and don't mind it being known that they have pretty underwear on.

So my smooth nude bras for wearing under light-coloured fabrics were replaced with lacy cream and blush pink bras (and matching/similar knickers). As with my nightwear shopping I had 'sexy and sophisticated' as essence words which helped me decide easily which made the cut and which didn't.

Home loungewear is another area where it's easy to slip into slob-out territory *and* it's just as easy to up your game at minimal cost.

In the winter I purchased a couple of pairs of clingy leggings (in black and navy) and alternated wearing those with two fine-knit merino tops (navy and grey) where the vee-necks were too low for wearing to work. They turned out to be perfect for home, worn with my leggings and a lacy bra underneath. Sexy and sophisticated – perfect!

In the summer I love to wear fine-cotton palazzo pants and a soft form-fitting tee-shirt in a colour that pairs well with the pants. I feel very 'spa luxe' and have two or three sets so there is always a clean outfit to put on. I change as soon as I get home from work which brings about a feminine and relaxed feeling; instantly the work day seems far behind me.

Feminine behaviour

I don't always manage it, but I try to keep my voice soft and light – no shrieking or bellowing. I try to be a good listener and also smile while I'm talking. Did you know that someone can tell you are smiling even when you're talking to them on the telephone and they can't see you? Smiling whilst talking changes your voice and you sound nicer. It's a habit of mine to smile when I am talking on the telephone now and, funnily enough, I've had many compliments from customers on my phone manner.

When I was a teenager, a beau asked me 'why I walk like a man' (such a charmer, I know) and I've never forgotten this. Some of us are natural stompers though, so I try to remember to keep my steps light and imagine a string pulling me up from the top of my head; this helps me walk and sit up straight without effort. It's fun to notice when I walk, that by lifting my feet *up* rather than putting them *down*, I walk in a more elegant way. Try it for yourself!

Doing these things, you will notice you feel much lighter and more refined and you'll look better too.

A feminine state of mind

I love to read feminine literature, have classical music playing in the background and generally do the sorts of things that put me in a ladylike state of mind. That way I don't have to consciously choose it, it just happens naturally.

Reading something traditional, particularly, puts me in a feminine state of mind. Books that some might consider old-fashioned from diverse authors such as Nancy Mitford, Louisa May Alcott, Laura Ingalls Wilder and Grace Livingston Hill all have such a gentle and chaste femininity about them that I can't help but feel soothed by a gentler time when I read their words.

If I'm in the mood for television instead, I indulge in *Downton Abbey*, *Mr Selfridge* or *The House of Eliott* (it's a little older than the first two but well worth searching out for a delightful story of two sisters making a go of their fashion business in 1920s London). I can relax and feel delightfully slothful but at the same time not dumb myself down; rather, I feel newly inspired to act and dress my most graceful self.

Remembering that I wish to be ladylike in all situations helps with a feminine state of mind too. I might be angry or upset but I can handle myself in a way that dignifies me instead of turning me into a screeching shrew.

In a disagreement the person with the quietest speaking voice always has the most power and it may also prevent you from getting so fired up that you say something you could later regret.

Enjoying feminine pursuits

I love the idea of feminine pursuits and even though I don't participate in all of the pastimes listed below currently, I know I will always have them available to me. I like to keep a big list and add to it when I hear appealing ideas or remember a hobby I loved as a child; then I always have inspiration to hand if I want to investigate something new.

Here are my favourite feminine pursuits that I wish to include in my life:

Playing the piano
Needlepoint
Knitting, crochet and sewing
Designing my own bespoke perfect capsule clothing collection
Spinning wool
Reading the classics
Writing for my own pleasure and to publish
Studying art history
Painting in watercolours (after reading Barbara Barry's 'Around Beauty' book)
Flower arranging

I often think I would have been excellent as the elite country house lady who didn't have to go to school, instead spending her days learning skills such as those included in the list above.

I don't know if I would have enjoyed the reality though because I value my education and like to make my own money. We have the best of both worlds these days, since we can be of the world *and* we can be that lady of culture and leisure in our free time.

Whenever I complain to myself that I don't have time to indulge in all the feminine pastimes I love, I remind myself that I could participate in all of these hobbies if I would address the time-frittering habits of watching television and mindless Internet browsing, by confining them to their proper, contained, space.

I'd then have plenty of time to expand my mind with cultured interests and this list reminds me of my deeper wishes.

Being strong in your femininity

Being feminine does not mean being weak or a pushover. My ideal chic female actually has great strength and capability alongside her gifts for being soft, kind and gentle. Some talk about a goddess energy which is similar. The feminine ideal I like to channel is sure of herself and decisive; she does what needs to be done, however she does it in a mannerly and gracious way.

A colleague I worked alongside for a number of years unwittingly demonstrated how this was done. If she wasn't pleased or wanted to change the way something was, she didn't complain or sulk, but rather cajoled and joked around with our boss in a charming and light-hearted way. It used to drive me nuts because 'she was letting him get away with it' but looking back I can see she had developed powerful feminine skills, whether she was aware of this or not.

There are many famous examples of strong,

feminine women too. One that comes to mind is Queen Elizabeth of England. She is a figurehead so doesn't actually run the country, however the Queen holds a tremendous amount of power and handles important documents almost every day. She takes her role extremely seriously too.

She comes across as warm and personable yet everyone who comes into contact with her is respectful and keeps their distance – it's almost as if she has a protective forcefield surrounding her, which she herself keeps in place. I've watched a couple of documentaries on Queen Elizabeth and from them have learnt a lot about the chic attributes of being feminine, capable and strong.

Thirty Chic Days inspirational ideas:

Ask yourself if you have been neglecting your feminine side lately. Make a list of ideas – big or small – that you can do to **bring femininity back into your life**. Some that come to mind for me are:

Wearing more colour around my face, either in tops or scarves by choosing colours that illuminate my skin-tone. I always feel more feminine when I wear colour alongside my black/navy/grey (as much as I love neutrals and yes, they do form the basis of my wardrobe).

Being softer in the way I speak – I decided I would walk to the room my husband was in instead of calling out. Half the time he wouldn't hear me anyway and I'd have to yell even louder. I did not feel like the feminine goddess I knew I was whilst shouting down the hall.

Enjoying the time it takes to **put on light, flattering makeup** and doing my hair in a becoming way, instead of resenting the time 'wasted' and rushing things. It takes all of ten minutes to put on a little makeup and another five minutes to fix my hair; I feel much better all day than if I hadn't bothered.

Wearing fragrance – I love perfume so much that I don't feel dressed if I'm not wearing any. You may not be a perfume person but even a fragranced body lotion is lovely.

Keeping up my grooming. As with hair and makeup, it takes minimal time to shave my legs, apply a face mask every once in a while or use my exfoliating gloves in the shower, but it always makes me feel more cared for and like I matter. I'm giving myself the gift of time and attention which feels great; if I want to go all out I have a spa evening or morning and do everything at once.

Keeping a pleasant expression on my face. This one might sound a bit funny to you but I've noticed it on others so I've been cultivating it for myself. Most people's resting face actually looks quite sour, mine included. If you think you look normal, you probably look grumpy. I've heard that as we age our mouths naturally turn down at the corners, so to look at least neutral we have to feel like we have a small smile on the corner of our lips.

If that sounds like it's too much effort, be assured it will become habitual after a while. As a bonus, anything physical like this also has mental benefits. It's a proven fact that if you smile you will start to feel happier, so it's an added advantage to looking approachable and pleasant.

Keeping my thoughts positive as well as being less critical and judgemental. I used to criticise and judge a lot, both out loud and in my head, but I found more and more that it made me feel yucky. Hearing others do the same thing made me aware that it makes the person making those observations look bad, not the person they're talking about – so I made a decision to delete this from my life. I'm not perfect by any stretch but being conscious of it means I'm a lot better – and happier and nicer – than I was. What you focus on grows so it feels wonderful to focus on what's good.

Playing background music – hotel-lobby-style piano or soothing classical adagios relax me and put me in a feminine state of mind. If I want to feel sophisticated and sensual I'll play Buddha Bar or Hôtel Costes which instantly transports me to a dimly-lit sexy little bar in Paris. Music is such a mood enhancer so pick your favourites and make yourself a few feminine playlists for different moods – deep and sexy, playful and carefree, empowered and rock on. The list is endless.

Day 14
Design the life of your dreams

Imagine your ideal and most fabulous dream life. If you won the lottery and had millions deposited into your bank account, how would you live and what would you do to fill the day? Would you still go to the same job or would you quit to start a business or form a charity to benefit the cause most important to you?

How would you spend a typical day with unlimited cash in the bank? Think big thoughts and let that be your guide as you consider what resonates most with you. Each of us only gets one shot at this life and every day time ticks on. Don't let that thought depress you though; instead let it inspire you to live your life with purpose and intention.

Don't let days, months and years go by on auto-pilot. To steer your life in the direction of your dreams, find yourself a pen and paper, a stylish notebook or a ring binder with loose pages. I prefer a ring binder because then I don't feel frozen about putting notes down. A pretty bound-notebook seems so final; I save these for inspiring quotes – you may be more daring than me however.

Start with a simple list

A great place to start is by listing categories – include details on how your ideal day would be spent, what your career would be, how you would look, where would you live? Really go into detail including all the facets that are important to you.

It might be a story or it could be a series of bullet points; when you have finished, put it away for a short while. When you come back to it, does it feel exciting to you or were you writing what you thought you should?

Dream about your ideal life and don't hold back. No-one else needs to see it, so include specifics you may feel self-conscious revealing to anyone else. They can be big parts of the plan or tiny details you want to incorporate into your everyday life... these delicious notes are just for you.

When you write ideas down quickly, they will come from the heart and cause you to recognise a little lift of excitement inside when you re-read them. Do not be tempted to think about your answers too much as this means they will come from the head – you won't be nearly so charmed by those suggestions.

Think about words that make you feel good and note

those down too. The kinds of words that inspire me, and which I desire to infuse into my life are ones such as: beauty, peace, harmony, serenity, tranquility, elegance, high style, sophistication, chic, refinement, authentic, quiet, simple, healthy, low-stress and low-maintenance.

Use *your* words as a touchstone to keep the focus on what you value and how you want to live.

Don't be swayed by others. This is your life and the only one who gets to choose the details is you. If you should choose to live in a romantic rather than a perfunctory fashion, whose business is that?

If people think you are shallow or silly for choosing French bread to go with your lunch instead of a slice of square white bread from a plastic bag, that's their problem. If you don't tell people what you're doing and make it look like you are having fun living your life (because you are), they will be drawn to that.

A friend of mine came into work so we could eat our lunch together one day. She brought with her a prepared salad complete with protein, dressing in a container, a tiny coffee plunger (French Press) and an even tinier container of freshly ground coffee to brew.

I took notice of this and it came off as very 'together'. She is a supremely stylish person who also likes good food, so naturally travelling with a one-cup coffee maker and home-made appetising looking salad was something she would do. What I have also realised is that she made time for both her health and her pleasure by creating a portable picnic.

Embrace the size of your life

I have made peace with the fact that I don't want a great big flashy life. At some stage I realised I crave a quiet and simple life which meant I no longer stressed myself with thoughts of 'shouldn't I want more?'

One of my personal favourite posts from my blog *How to be Chic* is called *Living a Small Life* where I wrote about this very thing. That was a few years ago but to be honest I still struggle with it sometimes, mostly, I admit when I see celebrities and larger-than-life high flyers. For some reason they trigger me and it makes me think I should want to be like them. I often wonder where unhelpful beliefs like that come from.

I then go through the familiar thought route of: but they may not be any happier than me, often people who look like they have everything carry tons of debt because they're spending a lot and so it goes on. It's because I am comparing myself with others, which never feels good, does it?

What helps at those times is for me to redo the exercise of first defining and then embracing the size of my life. What do I need to feel good? How big a house? How many friends? Maybe I am isolating myself at the moment, so why not make contact with a friend and go visit them?

Having a good tidy at home also helps with this funk. It's usually when I've been too busy or distracted to keep my house in order that feelings of inadequacy and overwhelm creep up on me. After a few hours of focused effort to clean, tidy and organise I'm feeling even better than if I'd had a massage or facial. Plus, my *home therapy* sessions are completely free (priceless in fact).

Decide on your version of a chic life

When I left home and started making my own way in the world on my modest wage, I'd dream about what I could have when I was older and more financially secure. As I walked through the glossy beauty counters at our local department store, I imagined the future me with a glamorous bathroom displaying my bounty of high-end products with their heavy glass bottles and polished gold lids.

Twenty-five years later when I could afford premium cosmetics without hardship, I discovered with surprise that I don't actually want them. I'm happy with lower priced and natural skincare brands.

At first I was confused but then I realised this was me actively deciding how *my* 'chic life' looked down to every last detail, rather than what others may choose. I was also giving myself permission to change as I grew older, not sticking rigidly to past ways of thinking. It makes sense then that I give myself full permission to change my mind to something different at any time in the future. I can love what I love now, but know that it doesn't have to be forever.

A chic life is not a cookie-cutter checklist with the usual entries you'd think about associating the word *chic* with, such as expensive sunglasses, the latest 'it' hairstyle or dressing like Audrey Hepburn. Yes, it can be all of those things, but it doesn't stop there. You can tailor it to suit yourself and be exactly the kind of chic person you want to be.

For example, the first image that comes to mind if I think about a chic woman is of a thin lady in her Chanel tweed suit out to lunch, then shopping for the rest of the afternoon – 'mwah mwah, darling'. That is so not me!

I am hereby reclaiming my own personal definition of *chic*. I am:

Chic and down-to-earth
Chic and thrifty
Chic and a casual dresser
Chic and practical
Chic and a homebody
Chic and an introvert who loves alone time
Chic and a keen knitter
Chic with a simple and classic wardrobe
Chic in light makeup
Chic with easy-care hair

Why not ask yourself what your chic life looks like?

Don't be afraid of big decisions

Looking back over my adult years, it has been the major decisions which have changed the shape and direction of my life. With some of those decisions I was merely following along after someone else, however the decisions I'm proudest of are the ones I made entirely on my own.

I moved to the big city when I found myself divorced at thirty, rediscovering my inner party girl and what made me happy.

I had braces fitted on my teeth at thirty-one for minor shifting that had bothered me for years (one of the best decisions I ever made – I love my teeth now).

Eighteen months after I met and moved in with my boyfriend, he opened a shoe store. Not long after that I left my office job to join him there. Eleven years later (and now he's my husband) we're still happily in business together.

In my early forties I read a book which, even though I didn't realise it at the time, made me to decide to stop drinking alcohol (it's called *No More Hangovers* by Allen Carr if you're interested). Four years on and I'm still loving that decision; I didn't realise it would be such a fateful day when I came across this book at my local library.

There are many important decisions you may put off, when in fact they could be beneficial to your health and wellbeing. Sometimes you hesitate because of what others might think, other times it could simply be the powerful force of inertia. Here are a few examples:

- Quitting a social club that has become more of an obligation and a drain on your time – you keep going out of habit and not wanting to let people down but it's not really you anymore.
- Joining a weight loss programme or deciding to become healthier – you are worried that you might alienate your other half or friends that you socialise with.
- Deciding to cut down on television watching in favour of reading, exercise, garden work or a creative hobby.
- Changing jobs, starting a new career, going back to school or leaving your job to start your own business.
- Doing something radically different with your hair or updating your image.
- Taking up something you've always wanted to do such as learning an instrument or enrolling in a night class.

What does this bring up for you? What's the first thought that popped into your mind?

Thirty Chic Days inspirational ideas:

One evening after dinner, when the kitchen is tidied and the house is quiet, take yourself off to your bedroom earlier than your normal bedtime and lie on the bed with a notepad. **Start your perfect life notes**. Early morning is another good time to do this, either on the computer or on paper. Password-protect your computer file if you want, then you won't censor yourself thinking 'what if someone else reads this and laughs at me?'

Come up with **twenty words you would like to describe your ideal life**. Use these words as guidelines and refer to them often.

Carry a small notebook in your handbag for writing ideas on the go, as you are inspired by others' actions and also to capture chic brainwaves while they are fresh. In addition, note down ways you *don't* want to be, then take the opposite as a positive action.

Dream big and think **'what would I do if I could do anything in the world with no limitations or consequences?'** Let that be your question as you fall asleep at night and look forward to the wonderful dreams that will follow.

Day 15
Cultivate serenity and calmness in your life

People often comment that I seem composed and tranquil and it's true, most of the time I am. It's not an accident though; every day I make a conscious decision to live a simple and low-key life. Something that has helped me feel happy and joyful on a day-to-day basis is my ongoing project of cultivating calmness. By removing myself from stressful situations, both big and small, I live a life that I love.

It first comes down to a decision. If life feels out of control and chaotic, think to yourself 'I want a peaceful life, so what do I have to do to achieve that?' Asking this question helps you look for ways to simplify your life for serenity.

There will always be situations and people to deal with that are the opposite of calm, but, if you have a harmonious life to begin with, they are so much more manageable.

Decide to be calm

My tranquil life started with a wish – I desired to live in a peaceful and simple way. I value a routine and comfortable home life which is quiet in both thought and action. I chose a wonderful man to share my life with; I couldn't be in a relationship full of drama and tenseness – I am *not* a girl who thrives on this. If one of us isn't happy about something, we bring it up straight away (and it's never anything big). We both agreed that we don't like conflict and we love to live in an easy-going and relaxed manner.

In our business, we deal with our customers similarly. We like to give them the benefit of the doubt because most people are reasonable and honest. There is the odd person you're not going to win with no matter what, so you may as well give them what they want, sending them on their way with love. It's not worth either our worry or them badmouthing us.

Thankfully, these types are a tiny percentage; for the most part our customers are lovely people who appreciate the service we give, sometimes even ending up being friends. We've had customers bring us home-baking, flowers, wine and small gifts. It goes both ways – we endeavour to be friendly, open and welcoming and we find most people respond in kind.

Do things quietly

Did you know that *any* noise registers on your subconscious? Apparently people who live next to busy streets or in a big city have slightly higher stress levels than those who live in a quiet street or a small town. This is because the constant hum of traffic is noticed by your mind which not only raises cortisol (stress hormone) levels but also uses up your energy – like a slow leak. This explains why you can feel exhausted after a long telephone call or a visit to a noisy mall. It's all that *listening*, whether it's voluntary or involuntary.

When I am at home I like to move quietly too. I close doors, drawers and cupboards quietly. Habitually, I walk as quietly as I can – stomping feet are neither chic nor calming. I play music softly. Very rarely, I might turn the volume up but mostly I prefer softness.

I even sit down 'quietly' most of the time, deliberately using my muscles to lower myself onto the sofa or chair rather than flopping down. This is quiet in a different way to sound – it's a quietness of movement which is good for you as well – you're using your small muscles, not only your big ones.

I started seeing a Reiki chiropractor about a sore shoulder and he would always give me 'homework' when I left after a treatment. Often it was along the lines of:

'Think smooth and graceful this week, Fiona'
'Be strong and supple'

'Use your small muscles'

Having these guidelines in my mind helped me move in a more elegant way (my shoulder is much better now too).

Unsubscribe

I belong to only a handful of shopping mailing lists – it is in single digits. Sure, it's easy to delete an email or throw away a catalogue, but I took it one step further, cutting them off at the source. That way they don't even enter my mind space.

I used to sign up for *everything* and even if I rarely bought from that store I'd still read their catalogues. One day I realised they were taking up real estate in my brain which was stopping me from focusing on creating my life, because I'd been distracted by a pretty duvet cover set or a cosmetics clearance sale.

Mailing lists for shops are, for the most part, designed to sell you something whether it's on email or in the post. Since I unsubscribed from 95% of the emails I used to receive, keeping only my absolute favourites, my inbox is manageable and low-stress plus I am saving money. It's incredible how much you never knew you needed until you saw it was on sale. I am also not inundated with catalogues in my letterbox which has the same effect.

Unsubscribing from nearly everything might sound drastic to you, but think about it – do you really want constant mind-noise from marketers shouting for your attention? I don't, it doesn't align with my idea of a tranquil and minimalist life at all.

But how can you tell if you want to keep a subscription? It's easy. If you are keen to open something as soon as it arrives or you happily look forward to reading it at your next tea break, keep it. If you open it only to unbold it or even delete unread, why not unsubscribe instead? It's the same with catalogues in the post – if you consider throwing a catalogue into the recycling without reading it, unsubscribe.

Don't be concerned that you will miss out on a deal (that's what stopped me for a long time), you won't; nothing you needed anyway. Trust that you will find everything you want (and at the right price) without being bombarded by advertising. Even if you pay slightly more for something at a certain time, you will save *so much more* in the long run not being tempted by all that advertising.

Simplify the picture

Decluttering your home on a continuing basis is another way to cultivate calmness. Sometimes items are there simply because they're there and, when you take a look at that ornamental sculpted knick-knack, you might realise it was a gift to your ex-husband when he left a job which you somehow ended up with. Yes, this is a true story of mine. It was donated the very next trip to a charity shop.

By continually paring down items around our house, quantities are kept manageable making it easier to keep our home clean and tidy. A great way to see things that your eye may have become accustomed to rendering it invisible, is to take photos of each room and have a look at them on your computer. You will see your home with fresh eyes, in fact much like a visitor would.

In our living room, there are three small neat stacks of books and magazines on a wooden trunk behind one of our sofas. They contain both library items and current reading; the stacks are meant to be kept low and tidy. However, they can quickly become twice their height and messy when other items are 'temporarily' placed on top as well. I don't often notice how unpleasant this area gets but a photo does. I can then enjoy instant gratification by decluttering and tidying that one area, making the whole room look better.

Tidying 'hot spots' calms the mind because your eyes can rest as you move around your home. Your conscious mind might not notice everything, but your subconscious does which means it's kept busy – much like having too many apps open on your smartphone or tabs on your desktop browser. Keeping hot spots under control reduces mind clutter dramatically. This is why it feels so calming after you've organised an area.

Thirty Chic Days inspirational ideas:

Make a decision to be calm. I used to think that I could only have a calm and serene life if everything around me was peaceful. When I realised that I was the one dictating the feeling, things changed. If I am relying on the world around me to help me feel at peace, how unstable is that? I'd be like a tiny rowboat bobbing around on big waves with no control whatsoever.

Nowadays, I know that I can choose to feel composed even if there is chaos around me; *especially* if there is chaos around me. This approach serves me because I am also better able to handle situations.

You don't need to fly off the handle at every small thing, you can choose to laugh instead of becoming upset, you can decide on tranquility as your default way of being. It might feel foreign at first but you will quickly become used to it after realising it is a calmer way to live.

Tidy up all the little stressors in your life. When I examined all the small areas that were testing my patience, I found there were quite a few. I committed to cleaning them up and now when I notice something bothersome, I sort it.

Usually they are quick and easy fixes; if they are a little bigger they are well worth doing also. If an item is dirty, damaged or doesn't work properly then clean, fix or replace it. There is absolutely no reason why you should not have a life of ease and beauty.

Here are a few examples I experienced recently:

I bought a new kettle because I noticed ours (which was second-hand from a family member) was leaking water. I'm no scientist but I do know that water and electricity aren't a good mix, so that day I purchased a new kettle. It wasn't until I'd plugged it in to make myself tea that I realised how long we'd been putting up with the daily annoyance of an aging kettle with a cracked handle.

The second example is our car (which my husband and I share); it is more than ten years old but reliable and we love it. It had a problem with the paint job on the bonnet (hood) though which really bothered me. A few years back we noticed little patches of peeling colour. A car painter told us it was only cosmetic, that the peeling was probably the result of a poor previous repaint.

We plan to keep this car for many years so we investigated the cost of having the bonnet repainted. It was less than we anticipated so we booked the job. Our car looks wonderful now after its 'facelift'; every time I see it I'm glad we fixed it.

Sorting such concerns eliminates that tiny drag on daily life. Much like driving around with the handbrake on, it's not until you click it off that you realise the expenditure on your energy.

Put calming measures into place. Find areas in your life that compromise your tranquility. Common issues I can relate to are:

Meal planning
Keeping laundry up to date
Getting out of the house on time in the morning

For each item on your list, look specifically at that task to brainstorm ways you can make it easier on yourself. It might simply be a matter of getting into the habit of planning ahead, or you may wish to consider outsourcing some tasks.

For something like our laundry, I'm happy to do it myself, but if I leave it for a week I have to do two or three loads in a day. If I do a load every few days however, the job never gets too big.

My answer to this then, is to be aware of where we're at with laundry, checking the baskets often to make sure the level stays low. This solution sounds so basic, but I would honestly drift through the week wearing my clothes, then be surprised when my drawers were empty and the laundry hamper was full!

Day 16
Create a sanctuary at home

The concept of home as a sanctuary is one of my most comforting thoughts. Where else can you relax feeling safe, nourished and strengthened, knowing you are surrounded by your favourite people, pets and possessions. Home is a place to rejuvenate yourself and relax, tucked away from the busy world.

If you read the newspapers or watch the news (I've stopped doing both and have never felt better), you'll know there are many tragic stories. Even though there is little you can do to help, they affect you. This can produce a feeling of being unsettled yet behind your front door you can feel cosseted, refreshed and taken care of – even if it's only you there and no-one else.

For all of us homebodies, home is our favourite place to be; we put time and energy into creating a unique, warm environment to both express ourselves and unwind. We enjoy inviting family and friends around to share our space, feeling proud when our guests look contented and happy.

An oasis of calm

One of the best parts of being a grown-up is living in my own home, where it is entirely my choice how it looks and feels. Even if you're renting, you have total control over what goes into your space. When I was a child, the bedroom was my domain entirely; I was surrounded by my beloved books, toys and hobby materials.

It's no different today – I have sincere appreciation for a home that nurtures my husband and I; our home is an oasis of calm which supports our busy lives. To achieve this, I prefer to decorate in a palette of soothing neutrals and keep the decor quite minimal.

As well as creating a tranquil look to our home, I establish stillness in the way it feels and sounds. Music is played softly – if at all; the television is only on if I'm sitting in front of it. Television advertisements are never heard – they are either muted or fast-forwarded. Have you ever noticed how loud advertisements are compared with the programme or movie you are watching? Some of them practically yell at you.

I take the notion of serenity down to the tiniest detail; if I am purchasing, for example, a new washing basket, I choose the best from the options available – currently we have a white one. I couldn't handle a bright yellow or orange washing basket. Or a kitchen dishwashing brush? We have a black one (unlike the garish lilac I could have chosen).

If a product comes in an unappealing container, I decant it if it's on display.

I recently decluttered my tea-towels eliminating the unattractive ones. I still have more than enough but now I love every single one of them. Since the details matter, why not choose what you love so that everything blends together to create a pleasing environment.

Decorate in a way that makes you happy

Over the years I have torn out many magazine pages to create quite a comprehensive style file. I found I'd chosen a few different styles but not all of them were 'me'. I often saved feminine, frothy, shabby chic style images but, in our home, I'm not comfortable with that decor.

This exercise made me realise I could appreciate a style without having to live with it. After a few décor disasters I now know that rather than trying to pinpoint my style, it's best to choose items that make me feel happy, sparking excitement inside me; that way I create my own style which is a cohesive blend of different influences.

An amusing example of this was when we finally saved enough to purchase new sofas after using an elderly set for more than a decade. The new set was being custom-made by a local manufacturer; my husband and I both thought we wanted simple modern-style sofas that would provide a good foil to our gilt mirrors and fancy cushions.

The first sofa I set my eyes on in the showroom was tufted and traditional, *not* what we'd come for at all. 'That's the one, it's gorgeous', I said to my husband, only half seriously. We continued looking around the large room, sitting on different sofas considering the various arms, backs, legs and cushion types.

When it was time to leave and we were back at the door with the tufted fancy sofas, my husband said 'You really like those, don't you?' I nodded.

So that's how we arrived looking for 'plain, square-shaped' sofas and came out with a rather ornate pair instead. That was four years ago and we've loved them ever since (they totally blend in with our style too).

Pretend, for a moment, that your home is a bed-and-breakfast

Take a leaf out of the book of fine hotels and boutique accommodation by setting up your home as a place of ease, comfort and beauty to be enjoyed by happy guests. I've found having this thought in mind makes it easier to become motivated about tidying up.

It's also a great chance to look around to see where you can add a small table or cushion to make an area more inviting. Imagine you are inviting paying guests in; you will suddenly see your home through their eyes.

You could even give yourself a fake deadline – say to yourself they are 'checking in at 5pm'.

I've done this and it works (I should add here that it often takes me *a lot* to get going with housework). Before I know it, I'm up out of my seat whisking clutter away, taking out the rubbish and dusting. I notice the windows aren't that sparkling so a quick clean with window spray and they look much nicer. One thing leads to another and soon our home is clean, tidy and fragrant with a scented candle burning.

It actually *does* feel like someone is checking in – me! After a productive few hours, it's such a pleasure to have a shower and fix myself up; when I come back into the living area, I feel like I've just arrived as a guest. The energy is fresh and I am revitalised.

Surround yourself with comfort

There will be colours and textures that make you feel nurtured and cared for. For many of us, these will be calming neutrals where our eyes can rest, with accents of favourite colours here and there. Earth tones are soothing and greens are proven to have calming benefits.

The main thing is to surround yourself with colours that reflect your style, not only what is in fashion (unless you have fallen in love with them of course). It's fun to see what is new for the season and it's equally as fascinating to see how style file images you tore out a decade ago can still make you feel joyous.

Have textures around you that make you happy. I love our soft cotton dinner napkins and crisp cotton bedsheets, mohair and alpaca throw rugs. I like things to be washable as much as possible; it feels so good on a sunny day to have a 'big wash' where I launder the duvet covers, rugs and mattress protectors.

One tip I borrowed from a five-star hotel is to use zip-up quilted pillow protectors beneath pillow slips. I have a few sets so I can change them every week when I change the bedding. They are quite inexpensive to purchase and last for years. Not only do these keep your pillows nice, they make the pillows much loftier and more luxurious-feeling.

Pets included

In my book, a happy home includes companion animals. In my adult life I've had three 'sets' of pets sequentially – two rescue cats, one rescue poodle and now two rescue cats. During the short pet-free breaks in between I've pined for animal companionship – the house seems so empty without at least one.

Especially for those of us without children, pets bring a fulfilling quality to our lives. For families with young children, pets are valuable family members who teach kindness and responsibility as well as being a non-judgemental and unconditional friend.

The fun and laughter you gain from a pet is worth the admission (or pet food) cost alone. I have heard so many funny stories and have many of my own about just how nutty and humorous pets can be.

Our cats make my husband and I laugh every single day with their antics, that has to be good for our health. Today one of ours had hiccups after her dinner. Hiccups! I didn't think cats could get them but obviously they can. It was quite amusing (don't worry, they didn't last long).

The more attention you give to your pets, the more personable they become. A cat that is not spoken to or played with who has no toys and sleeps outside will not be as sociable as a cat who has more human interaction. Our spoilt two have a small basket of toys, sunny spots to nap in, a cosy bed at night and plenty of play time. We adore their company and they often seek us out too.

I'd also like to put in a little pitch about choosing a rescue cat or dog (as well as any other animal you'd like as a pet, not that I've heard of rescue fish though).

Please choose adoption over purchase. There are many wonderful personalities waiting out there for their chance at a loving 'forever home' and I promise you they will add so much enjoyment to your life.

Thirty Chic Days inspirational ideas:

Take a look at your home with the eyes of a visitor. What does it say about you? Is this what you want it to say? Taking digital photos of each room is a great way to see your home as it is. Our eyes tend to skip over piles of clutter, unsightly cords or storage containers whereas in a photo they are illuminated mercilessly. You can then do something about them; for instance, I've heard that lamp cords can be taped to table legs – such a simple and clever idea.

Taking care of the details around your home can result in a big shift in energy – you will find yourself feeling calmer without realising why.

Move furniture and artwork around if you can. Everything seems new and it's a great chance to have a good spring clean. You will appreciate your belongings all over again.

Day 17
Take exquisite care of your grooming

It's rare to come across a twenty-year-old with a less than youthful complexion. Fast forward thirty years though and there can be a big difference between faces of the same age. What we eat, how we care for our skin, our daily habits, even our thoughts all add up to what we see in the mirror each morning.

I have heard that it is common for French girls to be taken by their mothers to consult a skincare expert so they can learn how best to look after their complexions. I am fortunate that my mother showed me as a young teenager the importance of cleansing, toning and moisturising my skin twice a day.

Even if you think it's too late for you, even if you've *never* developed a skincare routine only using moisturiser sporadically, please hear me when I tell you *it's never too late to start*. Today is the perfect day to start taking better care of your skin; if you remind yourself to take a few minutes morning and night it will become a habit before too long.

This simple act of self-care reinforces that you are worth spending time on; it will likely flow into other areas of your life too. It also helps your well-being because you're taking a small, tranquil time-out twice a day. The accumulated effect of both relaxation and the topical treatment will ensure you look as rested and well as you can as you age.

The Evening Regime

One part of my daily grooming that I will never skip is my evening facial cleansing routine. Not only is it essential that you cleanse your face at night, but it's also calming and soothing which is a lovely way to wind down before you go to bed.

My cleansing routine starts with a basin full of very warm water. I pull my hair back from my face with a towelling headband and use a gentle creamy cleansing lotion which I massage all over my face. I prefer non-waterproof eye makeup which is easily melted away with the same cleanser. Occasionally when I've (mistakenly) purchased a waterproof mascara, I use olive oil to emulsify it before I cleanse.

After a few minutes of gentle massaging, I use a large-size facial tissue to wipe off the cleansing lotion. Beginning with my eyes, I gently use the tissue to wipe away all my eye makeup then move on to the rest of my face, using a clean part of the tissue as I go.

Once I have removed as much as I can, I use a cotton flannel face-cloth to remove the cleansing residue – first dipped in hot water then wrung out until it is almost dry. I swish the face flannel in the hot water to rinse and repeat my steamy face-cloth wash a couple more times. I love this part and my skin glows with pink happiness afterwards.

I also include my neck and décolletage in this routine – not with cleansing lotion but simply with the hot flannel as I'm washing my face.

Because my skin is still damp, I don't use toner at night, instead I go straight to whatever I'm putting on my skin. I don't always use the same product – one night it might be rosehip oil, moisturiser and eye cream. Another night I might feel like going minimal, smoothing over a little coconut oil and that's it.

None of my products are expensive with most coming from the supermarket, chemist or health food store. I don't stick to one brand and like to try new products from time to time.

Occasionally I won't wear any makeup if I'm having a pottering day at home, so my night-time routine doesn't require makeup removal. In this case, I will use a cotton makeup pad with a little squirt of cleansing water or toner tipped onto it to cleanse my face before going onto moisturising.

After I've moisturised my face I apply body cream or a thick body lotion to my neck (around the back of my neck as well), shoulders and décolletage.

Lastly I apply lip balm before moisturising my feet and hands. Then it's time to snuggle in with a book – divine!

The Morning Regime

I wash my face in the shower – I know some frown on this but I love the fresh feeling. I use either a tiny squirt of mild foaming cleanser or simply warm water. After my shower, I pat a few drops of toner onto my face (using my fingers) then apply my daily moisturiser. I like something lightweight so my skin doesn't look too shiny and it has to include sun protection – at least SPF15. I leave this to absorb while I eat my breakfast then apply my light daily makeup after I've had breakfast and brushed my teeth.

Before I leave the bathroom I apply body lotion. Many years ago I made the decision to moisturise my legs, feet, arms, stomach – basically every part of my body I can reach. Prior to this I only moisturised the lower half of my legs... sometimes.

It felt luxurious and indulgent to moisturise all over and really, it was an extra ten minutes of time once a day along with the minimal cost of body lotion. Some days I couldn't be bothered, some days I was running late but ninety-nine percent of the time I did it. Now it's one hundred percent of the time because it's a habit that I don't have to think about *and I love it*.

My skin feels smooth and looks well – my dear niece told me one day how nice my skin felt when she touched my arm. Bless!

Makeup

I adore makeup, not in the 'express yourself' theatrical sense, but rather in the 'add a natural glow and enhance your beauty' kind of way. I always start with a light liquid foundation, using as little as I can. Even when I don't think I've put on enough, by the time I give myself a light dusting of loose powder I look as made up as I want to.

I apply a small amount of blush or maybe a little bronzer if I'm in a summery mood (both non-sparkly) then choose a lip colour. Now that I am heading into *a certain age*, I find that lipstick in anything darker than a medium tone bleeds into the fine lines above my mouth. What I prefer to do instead is add a swipe of lipstick over lip balm for a sheer wash of colour or I apply lipstick lightly adding a dab of lip gloss on top.

Finally, I do my eyes. I go into detail in '*Day 4. Make up your eyes*' so I won't repeat myself here, except to say that I used to find doing my eye makeup so deathly boring that I'd skimp on the time needed (to my detriment since I have light-coloured eyelashes with not much natural definition around my eyes). Now that I'm in the habit, I love giving myself time to apply my eye makeup in a non-rushed way.

As with skincare, my cosmetics all tend to be low-cost mainstream brands. I find it interesting that in my twenties I often used high-end products; now, twenty years later when I probably have more disposable income, I prefer less expensive brands.

Either I am more easily pleased or the quality of cheaper brands has improved – perhaps it's a little bit of both.

Throughout the day

Small touch-ups throughout the day not only keep me looking fresh but also help me feel more pulled together and energised. I'm sure I am much more productive and positive on days when I have a few two-minute refreshes.

At work, I have a small kit which includes pressed powder and a fluffy brush, a few lipsticks and glosses, a fine comb for my eyebrows, a clean blusher brush to dust under my eyes in case any tiny flakes of mascara have fallen down, and a travel-size perfume.

For my hair, I have a can of hairspray, a hairbrush, fine brown hair elastics and light brown bobby pins.

With this little arsenal I check in with the mirror two, maybe three times in a typical work day, depending on how busy I am. Some days it might only be once, after lunch.

You might not need as much as I like to have available, but even if you simply take along the lip colour you're wearing that day and a tiny perfume spray, it gives you a boost.

Elegant nails

French women famously have very classic taste in nails either buffed natural with a healthy look, or short and polished red. I go through phases with my nails. They are always filed to an even length with neatly moisturised pushed-back cuticles, but I don't paint them all the time. When I do paint them, I like to have them quite short with one of my brights or darks (if I'm feeling fearless), or a soft ballet pink for a more classic look.

I tend to paint my toenails more in summer, and I love the look of a strong colour (with no sparkles or shimmer). During winter I leave the nails to breathe without polish. You may have noticed that when you wear nail polish constantly your nailbeds can yellow. Only time spent without nail polish will remedy that.

I apply hand lotion many times a day and have it stashed *everywhere* – by my bed, in the passenger car door, by the sofa, at each tap where I wash my hands, a tiny tube in my handbag and a dozen other places I'm sure.

Each is different because I enjoy different textures and scents. Some are lightweight and sink in quickly, others I put on at bedtime because they are much richer. If you get into the habit of applying hand lotion often, it will help not only your hands look nice, they will feel comfortable as well.

Thirty Chic Days inspirational ideas:

Go the extra mile in one aspect of your grooming today. It might be applying body lotion, washing your face at night or shaping and polishing your nails. Choose one and make it a habit, before moving onto another.

Instead of throwing your hair into a ponytail to get one more day out of the last shampoo (I'm definitely guilty of this), gift yourself the time to **wash and blow-dry** your hair. You'll have to budget an extra half-hour but you'll feel like a million dollars.

Have a spa day or spa evening where you leisurely do all of your grooming activities that often get put off – exfoliate your skin and shave your legs in the shower, smooth on heavenly scented creamy body lotion and apply a face mask while you relax with a glossy magazine or book and a steaming cup of herbal tea.

At a spa I visited once, tea was accompanied by a tiny dish with a few dates, dried apricots and raw nuts. I thought this was such a lovely idea, so now I do this too. It definitely feels different from grabbing a handful of nuts out of a bag from the fridge. You know how everything is done deliberately and with intention at a fancy spa? Try it for yourself at home and see how special it feels.

Start using **handcream** more if it's a neglected part of your body. Hands are washed many times a day and it's an old saying that you can tell the age of someone by the look of their hands. Hollywood actresses who may have had numerous facelifts can't hide their age when you see their hands.

Find a lotion that absorbs quickly so you don't mind using it often; push back your cuticles and enjoy massaging in the handcream. Don't forget to include your wrists.

Day 18
Little and often

If there exists a universal rule for life, it could well be *little and often*. Anything worth achieving is constructed step by step, brick by brick, habit by habit. We are the sum of our daily routines; these can be good practices that build us up or unhelpful, unconscious patterns that sabotage our efforts.

Anything we do regularly quickly becomes a subconscious habit. As we repeat tasks and thoughts, they become ingrained in our brains much like shortcuts across the grass on a walking route. It's easiest to turn to familiar thought routes which is why it's important to avoid training ourselves into bad habits. By the time we realise they are hindering our efforts towards a beautiful life, these fine threads of thought have turned into heavy chains which are holding us back.

The key to life

The reason so many diets fail is because they try to change our *entire* way of eating all at once. They also neglect to address our mindset; we think by cleaning out our kitchens and stocking only healthy foods that we will instantly become healthy eaters.

We need more. Our minds need to go on the journey too; they are far more powerful than we can imagine. If you have ever tried to use willpower to avoid your favourite unhealthy foods whilst on a diet, you will know how strong the subconscious is.

It's the same with any endeavour whether it's losing weight, decluttering at home or looking to reinvent ourselves on a milestone birthday. The way to change bad habits is to make small tweaks and incremental upgrades which let us become accustomed to our 'new normal' at a comfortable pace. Over time this adds up to a measurable and, more importantly, lasting outcome.

This will always be a part of my life, because I don't believe we are ever 'done'. I am always alert for ways that I can make my life happier, easier and more streamlined so that I have time and energy for the important things. Feeling bogged down by my own bad habits does not support this so I love finding areas where I can make fun and simple improvements.

I've heard it said that the trajectory of a boat is a great way to illustrate this – one small change in direction which is barely perceptible at the time eventually leads the vessel to sail into a completely different body of water. This is also true of addressing unhelpful habits tiny change by tiny change. By tweaking one small thing at a time we will be in new territory months – and years – from now.

Little and often in relationships

In the movies when a man gives his wife a huge bouquet of flowers or a gift of jewellery, it is often to show he is atoning for something. These grand gestures are supposed to make up for infidelity or neglect from someone who puts everything and everyone else before their other half.

Giving love and appreciation every day rather than as a grand gesture is the happiest way to go. My husband and I don't swap birthday or Christmas gifts which I am fully happy with (I think it was even my idea in the first place). I value everyday gestures more and I don't need a wrapped box to know that he loves me.

How do I show my appreciation to my husband? I'll always ask him how he slept, kiss him goodbye, say 'thank you' if he's going to work that day and I am not, as well as considering his feelings before I say something.

He is also a proponent of everyday appreciation and does the same for me in his own way. I'm not saying this to brag, but the reality is that we often put the most important person in our life last, expecting them to always be there. I can tell you from experience there is no guarantee of this.

Make your other half *want* to spend time with you by demonstrating every day that you care for their happiness and they will likely reciprocate.

The *little and often* beauty regime

Whenever someone exclaims that I can't be the age I am because of my complexion (I'm not sure if they're just saying it to be nice, but it's always pleasing to hear), my husband says to me afterwards 'they don't see how you are in the bathroom doing your skincare thing every night, that's why your skin is like it is'.

And it's true; I've had a skincare routine since I was a teenager. In '*Day 17. Take exquisite care of your grooming*', I go through my beauty regime in detail. It might sound like a lot but most of it is done on autopilot (enjoyable and relaxing autopilot might I add) so to me it's just something I do, much like brushing and flossing my teeth.

Coco Chanel famously said that a woman is born with her face at twenty but deserves it at fifty, which goes along with this. The good news is it's never too late to start caring for your skin.

A healthy diet when you think *little and often*

I have had more than my fair share of Mondays where I wake up determined to 'be skinny' and 'not eat anything unhealthy'. Of course that only lasts until lunchtime when I rebel against my strict thinking.

What changed things for me was making small tweaks, one at a time, to the areas I could see were problematic. In my mind, I'd step through my day anticipating the times when I could fall off the wagon. Over time I have successfully changed many of these habits which, in turn, has led to a happier and healthier me.

Little and often as it relates to exercise

As mentioned in '*Day 7. Honour your body with chic movement*', I changed from being a sporadic gym-goer to a consistent exerciser thanks to the *little and often* technique. For me going to the gym was a time-sucking chore which I did not enjoy. It's so boring to walk around on that same piece of carpet for an hour! I thought going for a long gung-ho power walk was the *only* acceptable alternative to a gym workout so I rarely went, because it seemed so macho and my energy was drained even thinking about it.

What changed all this, what made me love moving my body more, was giving myself permission to go for a short walk, maybe even in my normal everyday clothes rather than changing into exercise gear. I'd walk around the block during a break from work, walk to a nearby shopping area to do errands or to the supermarket close to our home. On a dedicated exercise walk if I wasn't feeling particularly motivated, I'd go slowly for only half an hour versus not going at all which is what I used to do. On days when I felt on top of the world, I'd power through my walk and felt like I could take on anything.

This has made me more consistent with exercise and it's a lasting change which makes me happy, since I know how vital daily movement is to my health.

Housekeeping, the *little and often* way

Little and often applies to housework too. Cultivating daily, weekly and monthly routines means nothing ever builds up. When I've been lazy with my housekeeping or simply in a busy time, I've often felt like retreating to the sofa with low-quality chocolate at the thought of all the tasks in front of me. There's only one way out though, pick a job and do it, then another and another. The way to avoid this happening in the first place is to do something *most* days – a load of laundry, clean the bathroom or change the bed.

Even if you have a cleaner, there is tidying to do so they can actually see the floor to vacuum. The lowest-stress ways of doing this are to pick up as you go, never leave a room without taking something with you (my mother used to go on about this; I can still hear her calling out to me 'don't leave empty-handed Fiona!') and deal with small jobs as you notice them.

Gardening and home maintenance also benefit from the *little and often* technique in a similar way.

Little and often as it applies to money

When I worked at an office job in the city, my lunch breaks were a fun time to stroll around the shops treating myself to inexpensive purchases to brighten up the day – not to mention buying my daily sushi lunch and coffee with an apricot almond muffin most mornings.

None of these purchases cost much individually however when I added them up (whilst wondering why I never seemed to be able to save any money) I was shocked at the monthly total – all those small amounts added up to *a lot*, especially when I didn't have much to show for it.

This example shows you how *little and often* can work to your detriment. I turned this around by doing different things in my lunch break. I still bought my lunch, but by cutting out all the unnecessary expenses, I was easily able to start saving money instead of handing over what felt like my entire paycheck to the credit card company every month.

Instead of walking into a bookstore for a browse, I'd walk to the library where I could choose a book for free. If I needed to purchase something, for example a new bra, I'd take one entire lunch break to be fitted and take my time making a good choice.

Sometimes I would still go for a walk to browse, but that lightbulb moment linking my mindless spending to no money for savings was all I needed to be content with a window-shop and a spritz of tester perfume before walking back to the office.

Tiny acorns

The examples above are a few illustrations of what can be achieved when you think *little and often.*

Many people, including myself once, believe that you have to take massive action to get benefits. This thought can make ambitions seem so overwhelming that we end up doing nothing. You will be pleased to know that it is just as often the small steps taken every day that earn big results. For instance:

- Make your coffee at home most days, having a treat coffee once a week rather than buying coffee every day. You'll have an extra $1,500+ to spend on an annual vacation, for Christmas shopping or to reduce debt.
- Cut out one daily habit such as learning to drink your tea or coffee without sugar to be effortlessly trimmer in a year's time.
- Write 150 words a day and at the end of the year you'll have written a full-length book.
- Walk twenty minutes a day to be fitter and lighter in a year without changing anything in your diet.
- Declutter five items each week from your home and you will have donated or thrown out 260 items in a year.

All of these daily actions sound so small and achievable

that you almost can't believe the payoff they're offering but it's true, they all work out. As human beings we are trained to look for the quick, easy and instant method. The *little and often* method is easy, but it's not quick which is perhaps where many of us fall down.

Then there are the less measurable actions that add up over time such as going into a certain age in good health because you have chosen to be smoke-free, eat healthily, exercise regularly and manage stress levels as much as you can.

Don't discount any action as being 'too small', for it could be there where real transformation takes place, seemingly without effort. Choose one thing and start today.

Thirty Chic Days inspirational ideas:

Pick a problem area in your diet and **work out a change plan**. One area of mine was drinks and snacks before dinner. I'd have a Diet Coke with a small bowl of potato chips (which often led to a second and third bowl). I changed the potato chips to something more stylish such as cheese and crackers.

The cheese and crackers didn't pair nearly so well with Diet Coke so I started drinking Perrier Lemon or San Pellegrino sparkling mineral water. Then I started having the sparkling mineral water with no snacks which meant I enjoyed my meals more (as well as cutting out unhelpful calories). Now I usually have a champagne flute of sparkling mineral water before dinner each night, with snacks only on weekends if at all.

Think about how much body movement you do and see if there is a way you can **add in something small**. In addition to walking, I dragged my once-used (literally!) yoga mat out of the storage cupboard and slid it under our bed.

Now, instead of waiting for that day when I will want to put on a forty-five-minute yoga DVD (it hasn't happened yet), I pull out the yoga mat and do five minutes of stretches with a few downward dogs as part of my winding down time at night. It's not a big production and it feels quite calming. Even if you've not done yoga before, downward dogs are easy to learn. Google or YouTube for an example.

Pick a grooming element to start doing more regularly. It could be deciding to use your exfoliating gloves or body brush twice a week, applying body lotion every day, or using your mud mask once a week. Sometimes I realise months have passed since I had a mask so I commit to applying one that night.

Write these in your daily planner if you want. I used to do this with weekly tasks such as a spa night or simple mud mask. I'd be reminded to do it *and* it was satisfying to tick off a job done.

Day 19

Socialise in a relaxed manner

I am naturally quite a reserved person. I used to keep to myself a lot when I was younger because I was scared of sounding silly when talking to others. I was sometimes called a snob or aloof and I used to feel uncomfortable in social occasions.

Gradually I found ways to be both more socially at ease and to enjoy meeting up with people without feeling anxious at get-togethers where there were lots of unknown people. It makes such a difference when you can relax and enjoy yourself instead of standing rigid with fear in anticipation of how an event might unfold.

Give a compliment

A useful icebreaker when you've just started talking to someone is to offer a genuine compliment on something they are wearing. I often compliment a man on his tie, watch or shoes if he looks sharp, or a female on her dress or jewellery. If someone is looking slimmer than they were, I tell them so. A fail-safe one to say to someone is that they 'look great' if they do.

One day I bumped into an old friend when I was out walking, she looked rested and radiant. When I said this to her, she was touched and told me about the rough time she'd been going through after a close family member had died. She was only starting to feel okay again so my comment gave her a real boost. She did look well so I'm glad I passed on my thoughts.

The opposite is true too, if you are chatting with someone who looks tired or as if they've put on weight, there is no need to mention that. Remember the old saying? *If you can't say something nice, don't say anything at all.* My mother drummed this into me from birth and it still bears remembering.

If you are visiting someone at their home, compliment them on their décor; when meeting a friend in a café you can say 'great choice, I love this café' or 'what a fabulous café, thank you for choosing it otherwise I mightn't have found out about it'. There is always something positive you can say – be that happy and upbeat person people love spending time with.

Most people remember kind words for a long time. I

can still remember compliments I received years ago which makes me think back with fondness towards the giver.

Niceness makes the world go 'round, that's my motto. There's no need to be clever or smart (as in funny) as I used to believe; you simply need to be nice, show an interest and not complain.

When I was in my mid-twenties, I was invited along to Toastmasters by a stylish young woman who was a few years older than me but light years ahead in career progression – she worked for a company that my employer dealt with. I was both flattered and terrified by her invitation.

You can't imagine the nervousness I felt heading to the first meeting that Thursday lunchtime and my horror at seeing older professionals, both male and female, sitting in a group with a lectern up the front.

I did it though, it didn't kill me and I remained a Toastmasters' member until I moved cities some years later. Even though I felt thrown in at the deep end, it was the making of me as I now feel more confident in social occasions or when speaking with customers and suppliers. If you feel like you could benefit, perhaps going to an organisation such as Toastmasters might help increase your confidence.

The most helpful piece of advice I was given about social situations is to think about things from the other person's point of view. They are probably feeling as unsure as you, thinking the same thoughts such as 'what if no-one wants to talk to me?'

When I have pushed myself to speak to others, I have been amazed to find they are invariably nice. I honestly half expected people to say 'what are you talking to me for?' but this has never happened.

Asking friendly questions and being a good listener are the secrets

I've found the easiest people to talk to ask me questions. So if you are stuck for something to say, ask questions rather than talk about yourself. Not only is this easier than thinking up something witty and funny, it is also polite. By being genuinely interested in others you'll find that they will like you more and you will get to know them better.

Questions such as 'how do you know the bride and groom/party girl?' are good lead-ins to more natural conversation. By having a few up your sleeve you'll never be left floundering. Some of my favourites ice-breakers include:

Do you have any vacations coming up?
Do you have any plans for Christmas/Easter/the school holidays?
How are your parents?
How are your children doing?
Have you seen any good movies lately?
Have you read any good books lately?
What's new with you?

What's been happening with you lately?

The last two are particularly useful when you are stuck for something to say but don't want to seem nosy. The fear of being intrusive used to prevent me from asking questions. Now I know it's all in the wording and how you ask.

I recall some years back being on the receiving end of two interrogations masquerading as small-talk. I felt like I was being attacked. The first time I answered all the questions truthfully, but by the fourth or fifth question I was becoming so heated that I blew my top in an unladylike outburst. I'm not proud of that but maybe this person learnt a lesson that day. I certainly did – both not to be that type of questioner and to answer in a way that didn't leave me feeling exposed. I've also learnt that it's not law to answer every question someone asks of you.

The second time I also answered the questions asked of me, but I felt violated as I'd given personal financial information. Both these instances were around the same time and I'm thankful to say I haven't had such situations since... or maybe I'm more skilled now in steering the conversation.

When you don't want to answer someone's too-personal questions without seeming rude (isn't that funny, *you* feel like the rude one when *they're* the ones poking and prying), here are a few responses:

I don't remember, oh well, it's not that important
How interesting, why do you ask that?
Why do you need to know that?
Um, maybe you'd better ask X about that, if you need to know

And my personal favourites?

A quizzical look with head tilt whilst you say nothing at all
A small smile then silence, waiting for them to dig themselves in further

That may give them the hint.

The secret to small-talk is not so much knowing what to say but knowing when to listen (hint: it's a lot more than you speak).

One component of having charisma is being a good listener; another factor is making the conversation about the other person, not yourself. Both tie into being relaxed and successful when it comes to relating with others in a social setting.

Bill Clinton has been said to focus exclusively on the person he is talking to, even if they only connect for a brief time. The late Jacqueline Kennedy Onassis was known to be a good listener too and I've heard the same thing of her – that you felt like the only person in the room when she was talking to you.

Carry a relaxed attitude towards life

I've always loved the saying 'be hard to get but easy to live with'. It's stuck with me since I first heard it and I did that with my now-husband when we first met. I didn't smother him nor did I play games – I was straight-forward without scaring him off. When we'd been together for a while he told me that he remembered that and loved it.

Now that we've been together for over a decade, I hope he still thinks I'm easy-going as I certainly try to be – there is no way I want to be seen as a high-maintenance girl (it sounds like it's a compliment when men use this phrase but I promise you it's not).

I endeavour to be more mellow and less sensitive than I used to be – something my husband said to me a few years back initiated this. He said that because I am a person who notices every last detail and has high standards, when there is something that is not done well, the enjoyment is coloured for him because he knows I am not happy. He actually said that all he wants in life is for me to be happy.

When something small was not done well, he braced himself for me to be upset about it. I was such a princess! It may have been a terrible entree in a restaurant or bad service in a store. Often they weren't major issues, it's that I had a finely tuned eye for imperfections. Now that I realise this micro-scrutiny didn't make me happier, I've let the tuning soften, so that I notice the overall effect instead of every detail.

Life is much more tranquil and enjoyable because I focus on appreciating everything good, dialling down the times when my ideals are not met. When I think someone else hasn't reached my 'high standards', I look to myself. No-one is perfect, least of all me. I'm happy to say that this forgiving change has filtered down to how I treat myself as well.

Thirty Chic Days inspirational ideas:

Instead of dreading social occasions, think of them as **useful times to practice your skills** in the art of asking questions, listening and being interested in other people. Have a few questions ready and take note of questions that others ask – I've gathered a few of my own favourites this way.

Ask yourself honestly if your **standards are unreasonably high** and if you could relax them a little. Ease yourself when you're feeling uptight and wanting to complain over something tiny. Take a few deep breaths and imagine a drifting, floating feeling in your body then wonder to yourself 'will this matter in ten minutes' time? Ten days' time? Ten years' time?' If the answer to any of these questions is no, then let it go.

Day 20

Be your own chef

Picture yourself reading a book by the flickering fireplace in the sitting room of your French apartment. The dinner bell tinkles from the dining room so you put your book down and go on through. Your personal chef is setting down dishes covered with silver domes at the dining table; he bids you a cheery *bon appétit* as he disappears back into the kitchen.

You uncover your plate to reveal steamed fish with a light drizzle of lemon butter sauce next to a brightly coloured medley of vegetables which look and smell delicious. There is also a small bowl of deep green baby salad leaves tossed in vinaigrette, sprinkled with a few shaves of Parmesan cheese. *Parfait* (perfect)!

I've often thought how fabulous it would be to have a personal chef, someone who cooks all of my favourite dishes along with a few surprises. I'd never be tempted by fast food or snack food for dinner because a healthy, delicious meal would be presented to me three times a day.

My personal chef would refer to a list of my dietary requirements, fitness and health goals, likes and dislikes to assist with their job of creating a menu that is both nutritious and appetising. All I would have to do is order what I wanted and they would whisk away, gathering all the necessary ingredients for my meals over the next few days.

Create your personalised menu

Think about when you're sitting in a restaurant, menu in hand perusing your options. If it were me I'd be thinking 'what do I feel like today, what looks yummy, what sounds healthy, or what did I enjoy last time I was here?' Then I'd make my choice and order.

Why not create that same service at home? It's not only the part about having someone cook for me and wash up afterwards (although that *would* be nice); I often find the hardest part is dreaming up meal ideas, night after night. Reading through a restaurant menu gave me the idea to create our own household menu and become my own personal chef.

Sometimes we'd have home-cooked dinners that were quite inspired and delicious, but it would be a while before we had it again. My husband would say 'remember that amazing chorizo and smoked chicken pasta you made?' only to be met with a blank look from me.

By having a small notebook in the kitchen to jot down details of successful dinners we could build up our own 'private restaurant' menu, never being stuck for meal ideas again. I'd keep it as a living document because it would change depending on the season, likely evolving over time as well.

I could print a copy and keep it in a folder (instead of all those delivery menus) to help on days when neither of us can think what to cook.

I've bought food magazines and cookbooks before, but often I use a fraction of the recipes, for many reasons – I have hardly any of the ingredients, I don't eat one of the main ingredients, it's too hard to convert to gluten-free, I don't fancy it, the preparation time is too lengthy and the list goes on.

I don't work well with rigid menu plans but we mostly have similar meals on certain nights – for example, we'll often have a roast dinner on a Saturday night. For us, it would make sense to have our menu organised Monday to Thursday (we'd have a selection of quick and easy interchangeable meals on those nights), Friday (often homemade fish and chips), Saturday (a roast in the oven) and Sunday (comfort meals such as spaghetti bolognaise or another type of pasta).

I don't need menus for breakfast and lunch because we mostly eat the same each day – breakfast is fresh fruit with raw nuts and a café latte, lunch is a big salad in the summer or homemade soup and salad in the winter and maybe bought sushi rolls once a week. That means our household menu can focus on dinner.

Here's a sample of how we're eating at the moment:

Monday through to Thursday we mostly have oven-cooked meals with plenty of vegetables, such as:

Crumbed, baked chicken pieces with roasted potato, pumpkin, kumara (sweet potato), carrot and onion halves with steamed vegetables – broccoli, beans and cauliflower dressed with a splash of extra-virgin olive oil.

Homemade meatloaf (either chicken mince or beef mince) with the same roasted and steamed vegetables. I often make two meatloaves at a time. My husband and I eat half of one between us for dinner, we then have three other dinners that can go in the freezer. I serve our meatloaf with gravy or a sauce made from canned tomatoes.

When I use our freezer-meal meatloaf, I have two favourite ways to serve this:

Either – heat in the oven in a casserole dish with a lid. I use a can of diced tomatoes with the contents of a gravy packet stirred in. As it heats through the meatloaf becomes lovely and moist; the tomato gravy is divine poured over. Serve with baked potato and steamed vegetables.

Or – slice the meatloaf into three, pan-frying each side until heated (one slice for me, two for my husband). Serve with mashed potato, steamed vegetables and gravy.

Other weekday dinners include:

Chicken breast pan-fried, served with cheese sauce and steamed vegetables.

Beef casserole in the slow-cooker, served with mashed potato and steamed vegetables.

Lamb shanks in the slow-cooker, served with mashed potato and steamed vegetables.

In the summer we use the barbeque more; a favourite meal is fillet steak and mushrooms, with homemade fries and coleslaw or baby potatoes and green beans.

Friday

Homemade fish and chips. We buy fresh white fish to toss in seasoned breadcrumbs. Bake in the oven with sliced Agria (floury) potatoes sprayed or brushed with olive oil, sprinkled afterwards with seasoned salt. Serve with coleslaw or a simple green salad misted with vinaigrette (homemade in a spray bottle – equal parts extra virgin olive oil and balsamic vinegar).

Saturday

We often have a roast dinner such as chicken, lamb or beef with roasted and steamed vegetables. I make my own gravy with the pan juices; once I've taken the roast meat out of the oven, placed it on a chopping board and covered with foil to rest, I put the roast vegetables which have been cooking in the same pan into a smaller dish back into the turned-off oven to keep warm. I then tip out the fat from the roasting dish into a clean tin (usually a tomato tin I've saved). This tin goes into the fridge and is put out with the trash when it's full.

To make gravy I combine cold water with either cornflour or gravy mix, stirring into the pan which is heating on a stovetop element. The aroma of the pan is so good and this method makes the best gravy ever. Using a wooden spatula, I gently scrape off all of the caramelised roasty bits until they become part of the gravy. The added bonus is that the pan is cleaned as well.

Sunday

Sunday night is comfort food night. We might have a beef mince meal such as spaghetti bolognaise, shepherd's or cottage pie, nachos or homemade lasagne.

We also enjoy homemade crumbed chicken tenders (baked in the oven) with dipping sauces, baked potatoes topped with sour cream and butter, and a side of coleslaw.

As you can see, we like to cook in the oven a lot and there are a few reasons for this.

One, we both love the taste of oven-cooked food.

Two, oven-baked dinners are comforting and filling whilst still being quite healthy. We don't use a ton of oil in the roasting dish, just enough so the vegetables don't stick. If we're being extra healthy, we'll cut down on the carbs (potatoes and kumara) serving plenty of vegetables to enjoy with our lean protein. It also means we're not having pasta or rice too often.

Three, once you put dinner in the oven, it cooks itself so you can do something else for an hour until the buzzer rings meaning it's time to steam the green vegetables and serve up. I'm all about ease in the kitchen so if I can 'set and forget' there's much less chance I'll be tempted by takeout menus.

What would YOU like to have for dinner?

Being your own chef means you can tailor a menu to your household's own tastes. You might think the meals I have described in this chapter sound terrible, or you may have gathered a few ideas for yourself. What I do hope this chapter has provided is inspiration for you to start putting together *your* ideal menu.

Start with your favourite meals and your family's favourites. Think about what each family member would choose if it were their birthday and they had free rein to decide where to eat that evening. Another idea is to take note of what each of you orders when you go out.

These lines of enquiry could evolve into treat meal nights instead of less healthy fast food. You might have homemade pizza night with bowls of toppings to choose from, perhaps a homemade version of fried chicken, chips and coleslaw (it's easy to make a delicious coating for chicken pieces and oven-bake them along with sliced potato sprayed with oil) or a Thai-inspired stir-fry with loads of colourful vegetables in a peanut satay sauce.

Ask friends, colleagues and extended family the question 'what's your favourite go-to meal to cook on busy weeknights?' when you're chatting. It's quite illuminating because some out themselves as real foodies and you can pick up great meal ideas too.

Above all, look at creating your personal menu as a fun way to look forward to meals as a time of inspiration and nourishment. Keep it as a working document as there will always be new ideas you're adding and meals that you're tweaking as you cook them.

Thirty Chic Days inspirational ideas:

Make a list of your family's favourite meals to start creating a menu. You could even recreate the fanciful descriptions used by restaurants to make healthy meals sound more appealing to your family – really sell it to them! For fun, write the evening's menu on a blackboard like they do in French bistros.

Peruse restaurant menus if you need inspiration. Most restaurants post their menus online; it can be fun reading through them to choose something new to make. I find menus more useful than recipes when creating a meal because often I don't follow a recipe to the rule but I can use a menu as general inspiration.

Find homemade versions of your family's favourites, whether it's fast food or restaurant meals. If you need more guidance do an Internet search for a homemade version of a bought meal that you know your family loves.

Read the packets of ingredients you purchase. Often packets have a recipe on them; I have come across quite a few meal favourites this way. The most recent success was from a shredded Parmesan cheese packet where I learned how to cook a delicious carbonara – it was easier to make than I realised and tasted as if it could have come from our favourite Italian restaurant.

Day 21
Inspire yourself

If we're listening for clues as we go through life, we grow into more of who we already are. It's great to realise that we don't need to change ourselves to be happy, we simply need to peel away the layers that aren't us. Michelangelo, describing how he created his sculpture of David, said that he simply chipped away all the stone that wasn't David. Isn't that splendid? And we're the same.

I've made it part of my daily round to look at what makes me happy, what I could do better, how I can serve others in a way that thrills me along with all sorts of other interesting questions. I love to find new inspiration so that I'm growing, changing and loving my life; it's much more enjoyable than being stuck in a rut.

I try to make self-improvement I wish to do fun, simple and appealing. I sometimes find it hard to motivate myself in areas such as eating healthier or tidying the house for example, so I look for inspiration instead. When you're inspired to do something you can't wait to take action. It's the difference between pushing yourself towards something versus being pulled towards that same thing.

Feeling attracted to an outcome takes much less energy and effort, with the bonus that you're having fun instead of feeling like you're completing a chore. You're also likely to be efficient, getting more done in less time when you're excited about what you are doing.

Ask yourself good questions

Our minds have an interesting way of operating. If you ask yourself, 'why am I so fat?' or 'why can't I be bothered cleaning my house?', your brain will automatically get to work answering those questions for you. For the first question I might hear 'because you're piggy Fiona, you eat sugary snacks between meals every day', for the second my brain might say 'because you're a lazy tart'.

These are not useful answers as they won't make you feel any better *or* motivated to change. The way to use your mind for the best result is to ask yourself positively phrased questions.

How much better would it feel to ask yourself 'how can I be consistently slim in an easy, fun way?', or 'how can I make my home look divine in the shortest possible time?' These questions feel so much lighter; immediately your brain starts thinking of all the ways you can answer them.

Keeping your positively phrased question in mind makes it easier for you to start taking action, and it's only when we take action that things change. Unhelpful questions do nothing but keep us stuck in our self-perceived 'problem'.

The fabulousness of affirmations

Affirmations work in a similar way. We all have a pre-recorded way of thinking that we picked up when we were younger by listening to our parents or others around us; we're also shaped by experiences we've had. Some are useful, others are not. You can never empty all these beliefs from your mind, but you can overlay them with new thoughts which, if you tell yourself them consistently, will crowd out the old beliefs.

So instead of feeling frumpy and flabby, saying to myself 'I'm never going to be slim, I'm going to keep getting fatter and fatter as I get older and my metabolism starts to slow down like everyone says it will', it would be better to say the following instead: 'I am changing my size and shape. I am in complete control of the thoughts in my mind. I am in total control of everything I put into my mouth. Every year I become fitter and healthier'. Whenever the old thought comes up, I simply repeat my new affirmation over top of it. I'm the one in control.

It seems almost magical that since I first started practicing this, cravings for certain unchic, unhealthy foods – foods that I thought I'd never be free of – have simply fallen away. You have to experience this for yourself to believe it; I certainly didn't think it could be so easy. The great news is that you can do this with *anything* you feel is holding you back.

I also use the phrase 'I am safe today and always' when I'm feeling scared. If I've taken all practical steps to be safe but I still have fear in my mind, that's all it is – in my mind. Repeating 'I am safe today and always' as needed soothes my overactive thoughts.

The Twenty Ideas method

Another way to come up with creative, personalised ways to enjoy your life more is the Twenty Ideas method. I heard about it from author and speaker Brian Tracy, while he attributes it to author Earl Nightingale.

Say you want to lose weight but think it will be too hard, saying to yourself 'I can't be bothered, and what's the point of even trying because I don't want to give up my favourite foods'. That's not going to motivate you at all; any weight loss will probably be an uphill battle. Rephrasing that desire as a positive question turns into: 'How can I become slimmer in the easiest, quickest, most fun way possible?' Now, who wouldn't be drawn to that prospect?

Whenever we ask a question of ourselves, our mind immediately looks around to find answers to that question – it simply can't help itself; it's how our brain works. Asking a down-in-the-dumps question will give you similarly depressing answers, whereas an enthusiastic and jolly question will offer more enticing results.

Once you write down your question, don't stop answering until you reach twenty ideas. The first answers will come easily but as you get up to twenty, it may become more difficult. The last few could feel like trying to get blood out of a stone, but don't stop because those may be the ideas that are most fruitful, which could cause you to change something seemingly without effort; they could be the 'aha!' ideas. A tip if you are stuck: try taking the opposite of answers you already have and write those down as well.

Here's what I brainstormed with my weight loss question:

How can I become slimmer in the easiest, quickest, most fun way possible?

1. Make it fun to be slimmer by finding inspiring role models – celebrities or people I know
2. Feel empowered instead of deprived when I skip foods that I know aren't good for me

3. Focus on nourishing my body with gorgeously real foods instead of thinking about the unhealthy foods I can't have
4. Repeat affirmations to crowd out old, unhelpful ways of thinking
5. Declutter my home, starting with my kitchen
6. Declutter my wardrobe, keeping only what I feel amazing in
7. Line up great podcasts and audio books so I can't wait to go for a walk each day
8. Drink loads of water to hydrate my body – tick off ten big glasses every day
9. Make healthy food exciting by buying yummy salad ingredients
10. Visualise myself as slim and trim and know I am changing my size and shape to reflect that
11. Stock our pantry and fridge with healthy snacks such as raw almonds and other nuts, fresh fruit and sparkling mineral water
12. Tweak my meals so that the carbs are lower and the protein and good fats are higher
13. Make myself a recipe folder or notebook with appetising and healthy meal ideas
14. Create a list of 'takeout alternatives' which I can have as a treat meal instead of junk food
15. Have a few back-up meals in the freezer for busy days
16. Get lots of sleep – at least eight or nine hours
17. Commit to becoming healthier for good – my weight will follow

18. Don't buy foods that are my failing – if they're not in the house it's much more inconvenient for me to eat them
19. Tell myself that I am in complete control of my thoughts, I am in total control of what goes into my mouth so that cravings have no power over me
20. Prepare food ahead of time so it's ready at mealtimes, that way there's no barrier to healthy eating

This took me twenty minutes all up; I now have an appealing list of ideas that makes me feel inspired and optimistic.

Any project that you'd like to start, or a problem that is bugging you will seem much more manageable if you ask a good question then listen for the answers.

Why not dedicate a small notebook to your lists – the 'Twenty Ideas notebook'. Keep it with you for when you have somewhere to wait such as the dentist or on public transport.

Be authentically you

Think about those who inspire you – is it their uniqueness that appeals? Anyone who's done well for themselves invariably has their own way of expressing their style, often with a unique physical look. I'm thinking about people like Dita Von Teese, Rachel Zoe, Michael Bublé. And what about Pharrell Williams? Totally original. Each of these people took their gifts and strengths and mixed them in with their own style and taste.

I love to read about how Ralph Lauren started his business. He married creativity with his dreams and merged his fantasy way of living into reality. Some may say he isn't that person, that he's different to how he started. I say he was always that person and it was his surroundings which have changed to reflect this.

These days I'm more likely to ask myself what I desire than to copy those around me. If you gather together all the pieces you love, *really love*, in every area of your life it will all jell together to create your own personal style. It doesn't matter if parts are bad taste or kitsch; if you love something then own it. Remember the cool girl at school who always looked amazing and started all the new fads? Remember how everyone always copied what she did even if it was questionable? But she never copied anyone?

How do those people do that?

I think it's by being happy with their own ideas. By being happy to be themselves. You don't see the cool girl scanning everyone else to see what they're wearing. No, she's having fun; chatting, laughing and living her life.

Don't waste your time wishing you looked like someone else or lived their lifestyle. Focus on where you're at, appreciate it and build on it. Start from where you are and claim your unique aspect on life. Enjoy your obscure hobby, 'interesting' book choices and favoured décor style. It might cheer you to know that there will be people in your life who look to you and your style as inspiration. You have a valid point of view, as we all do, so celebrate it.

Thirty Chic Days inspirational ideas:

Rephrase questions so they inspire, rather than bring you down. Keep practicing this by noticing whenever you ask yourself questions that make you feel bad. Catch them and ask them in a nicer way (as if you were talking to your closest friend); with practice it will become your new normal to speak more positively. Our minds pick up everything so it's in our best interest to speak well to ourselves.

Create a few **affirmations** for yourself. This is as easy as writing down your desires in the present tense as if they were already true. For example, 'my desk at work is always tidy and clear', 'I love my clean and elegant home' or 'I am effortlessly at my perfect weight'.

Read your affirmation list two or three times a day so they sink in. Within a week you should find yourself acting differently, more aligned with your ideal self and it will almost seem like a miracle. Keep repeating your affirmations so they infuse themselves into your daily thoughts.

Have fun with the **Twenty Ideas method**. Brian Tracy noted when he was talking about this exercise that if you answered one question each day, at the end of the year you would have 7,300 new ideas. Do you think that would inspire you?

To get a head start, think of ten questions you'd love to excel in, master or find the answer to. Keep a running list in the back of your Twenty Ideas notebook, adding to them as you think of one. That way you'll never run out of inspiration and then, when you next go to brainstorm ideas you'll have a readymade list to choose a question from. Off the top of my head I'd ask myself:

How can I be more efficient at work?
How can I keep my desk clean and my work tidy?
How can I find time to regularly declutter hot spots?
How can I love healthy food more?
How can I find more time to read all my lovely books?
How can I make the most of the clothing I already own?
How can I fit regular and fun exercise into my day?
How can I get to bed earlier?
How can I feel relaxed, calm and happy as a default state of being?
How can I work three days a week instead of five?

You get the idea – your questions can be big or small, frivolous or deep. When you read back through them, notice when they make you feel good inside; you want more of those sorts of questions.

Day 22
Build rest and repose into your daily routine

Something I've learnt to do which has helped me tremendously in building a life that I love, is to realise that it is okay to rest. I used to feel guilty for not being busy all the time which meant my downtime was often coloured by guilt. I would never expect someone else to work without pause, but I wasn't applying that permission to myself.

Working full-on one hundred percent of the time is neither healthy nor reasonable yet some of us need to be reminded of that.

Resist the urge to rush

I often start my day off with a huge to-do list then panic that I'm not going to get it all done. I think to myself 'how fast can I get through all of this?' or 'I'm going to be exhausted at the end of the day'. That's hardly setting myself up for success, is it?

I have found it far more helpful – and productive – to trim my list down. All it takes is reading through and choosing the task that is the most important, then working on that until it is finished. I cross that task out, then choose the next most important task.

Some jobs I can dovetail in, such as sending an email at work because I may have to wait for a response, or putting on a load of washing at home. For the most part though, it's simply common sense to complete one task then the next.

It helps to focus on the task I'm doing, carrying it out in a measured, leisurely manner. I find I enjoy doing it more, I do a good job and the time spent isn't much more than if I was rushing through it.

It's when I feel pressured (by myself) that I procrastinate, finding other jobs that are much more 'important' to do.

Gifting myself the time to go through my list in an unhurried way means I find my day unfolds beautifully and I often get more done than I thought I would.

Sleep like a chic lady

When I burn the candle at both ends, it shows on my face and I feel it in my body. Sleep is the ultimate beauty elixir and *it is free*. It is smart – not self-indulgent – to make quality sleep a priority. Don't believe those who tell you they regularly get by on four or five hours a night; I just don't believe it's possible.

Early to bed and early to rise is a time-old saying for good reason. An hour before midnight is worth two after, so remember this when choosing your sleep and rising times. Going to bed well before midnight means you won't mind rising early. Maybe I've turned into a morning person but I cannot understand why someone would want to stay up late and sleep in late; it doesn't sound appealing to me, but I can appreciate that we're all different.

My preferred time to have lights out is 10pm; I like to be in bed reading by 9.30pm. I always get up at 6am so that means I have eight hours of rest. In the winter when it's darker much earlier, I sometimes find myself getting ready for bed about 8.30pm with lights out at 9.15pm. I never thought I'd see the day when I considered this sort of behaviour to be pure luxury (especially in my younger days of going out socialising until 1am) but here we are, that day has arrived and I couldn't be happier about it.

Going to bed early can help you be slim

It's an often quoted fact that the later you go to bed the fatter you are likely to be. There seems to be a couple of factors at play – staying up late makes you feel tired the next day, so you look for a high-energy fix to keep you going. In addition, many of the body's repair and biological functions happen at night when you are resting; if you aren't asleep at the time they happen, you can miss out.

I also find that if I'm still up around 11pm I get a second appetite; any extra food adds unnecessary calories I wouldn't have had if I were asleep.

If I don't have a definite turning-in time, it's too easy to potter around doing nothing in particular, or stay glued to a screen and before I know it I'm tired and it's late. Then in the morning it's tempting to sleep in, however moving sleep and wake-up times around produces a form of jet-lag that makes you feel rubbish, craving pick-me-up carbs the next day.

Choose rising and sleeping times that work with your lifestyle, then stick with them no matter what. When I first started being stricter with these times it was difficult for me to get out of bed at 6am on a rainy Saturday when I had nowhere to be, but now that it's a habit I absolutely love it.

Honouring set rising and sleeping times will keep you youthful, fresh-faced and slimmer for longer. You will also not believe the general improvement in your mood and outlook.

Enjoy boudoir time in the evening

A leisurely evening routine is one of my favourite ways to wind down before bed, giving myself the best chance of a good night's sleep. I might start out by making an herbal tea to take to our bedroom, where I'll choose soothing reading material to enjoy for half an hour while relaxing on the bed.

It's nice to start with a clean, tidy bedroom where the bed has been made in the morning. If your bed is not made, take a few minutes to straighten the sheets and duvet, fold back the top sheet and plump up your pillows.

I like to have the overhead lights off, switching on the lamps either side of the bed. Bedside lamps are a worthwhile purchase as they cast a soft glow which feels more conducive to calming boudoir time.

Our bedside lamps weren't expensive at all; they are a cream-coloured simple style costing only $12 each at a discount store. One day it may be nice to have high-end lamps, but for now these do the job perfectly. I use low wattage bulbs so the light is not too bright.

Before I start reading with my herbal tea, I wash my face then might use this time to exfoliate and paint on a mask to purify my skin while I read.

In my bedroom I have a small bookshelf with my favourite French chic, positive thinking and spiritual books. There is also a hardcover notebook where I write my favourite quotes and passages which is a nice reading option at this time as well. I choose one of these books and enjoy it while I sip my tea.

Re-reading a few pages from my quote journal or a chapter of a favourite book puts me in a positive and relaxed frame of mind, washing away the day's minor annoyances; I can feel myself sinking into the quietude which allows me to enjoy a peaceful night's sleep.

If you have trouble sleeping

Many of us have periods of time when we have trouble getting to sleep or staying asleep. When I'd had sugary foods after dinner (or alcohol, when I used to drink), I found that I would be restless during the night – this is associated with spikes and falls in blood sugar which wakes you.

Some people have issues with caffeine so they don't drink it after dinner or even after lunch. Caffeine doesn't bother me and I only have one or two coffees a day. It's what we're sensitive to and what affects us that we should look to when investigating sleep issues.

You may wish to consider the traditional Chinese medicine 'Meridian Clock' – every two hours throughout the day or evening one of our body organs is going through an active cleansing process. For example, the liver is most active between 1-3am, so if you are regularly waking up at that time it might be worth looking at blood tests focused on your liver to research how you can better look after it.

Turning off screens (computer screens are brightest and wake up your brain) a few hours before bed is a good idea, as is indulging in relaxing activities such as self-care and reading. All are aids to boosting tranquility at bedtime.

Have a day of rest and relaxation

One of my favourite no-cost luxurious 'treats' is to have a day at home by myself with no particular jobs planned. I might do a load of washing or have a tidy up but, for the most part, I can do exactly as I please.

I might go for a walk then have a lazy breakfast watching a movie whilst knitting. I may do some writing but not because I need to get anything finished – I can enjoy doodling around having creative dreamtime.

Another option is a home spa 'appointment' where I enjoy a nice long hot shower, shave my legs, deep-condition my hair and use my exfoliating gloves all over. Afterwards I'll smother myself in scented body lotion and choose a pretty perfume. Dressing in clean and comfortable clothing, maybe leggings with a long-sleeved tee-shirt, I can then continue my day of luxury.

Later in the day I'll start preparing dinner or to be extra decadent I could order in an Indian meal so I don't even have to cook. That really would top off a day of ease.

What are some other ways to spend a soothing and restorative day at home?

- Read a fiction book (if it's cooler weather, I'll snuggle up in a throw rug on the sofa or bed)
- Start a small sewing project that I can finish in a day

- Reorganise my bookshelves and browse through my favourite books at the same time
- Find a new dinner recipe or do some baking
- Have a play around with my perfumes, wrapping papers and cards, knitting yarn or fabrics
- Declutter and organise an area – maybe my drawers, closet, pantry or sewing room
- Clean and organise my makeup
- Ring a family member for a chat
- Email a friend I haven't talked to in a while
- Read through my inspirational notebooks and find something to inspire a new project
- Write some of my current book
- Brainstorm blog post ideas
- Lie in the sun with the cats
- Go for a walk
- Take ages blow-drying and straightening my hair so it's perfect and hairdresser-worthy
- Choose one of my beautiful large-format picture books to browse through
- Scout around for items to donate – there's always something
- Fluff up the living area to make it pretty – light a candle and straighten up the room as if I am expecting guests
- Journal with paper and pen
- Take a nap
- Research and plan a holiday to look forward to

- Dream of the future – make goal lists of my desires to see if any of them (why not all?) are realistic for me to aim for

I wouldn't do *all* of these things in one day of course, but even reading through this list feels calming and peaceful. It's fun to pick a few ideas to indulge in on a day at home.

Thirty Chic Days inspirational ideas:

Decide how many hours of sleep per night would be ideal for you. May I suggest in the region of seven to nine hours? Based on what time you want to get up in the morning, choose your new bedtime. Ensure you get up early enough in the morning to do everything you need to do and have a bit of time up your sleeve to preserve your serenity.

Tell your other half that you are going to **start going to bed earlier** because you feel you don't get enough sleep at the moment. You may even need to move dinnertime to an earlier spot. We usually have dinner ready to eat around 7pm-7.30pm. If it is later for any reason, we might not eat until 8pm plus; when I want to start heading off to wash my face around 9pm there's not enough time to relax and digest. I end up going to bed later on those nights when I'd much rather go to bed earlier.

Get up in the morning as soon as your alarm goes off. It might feel luxurious to drift back to sleep but you will wake up feeling worse, and with less time to get everything done before you leave for work. Or, on the weekend, it might be an hour or more before you wake up after pushing the snooze button which means you will not feel well for having gone back to sleep. When I do this I usually end up with a headache.

Make yourself a list of twenty ways you would spend a rest/spa day at home. It was quite a mission to come up with my list but I kept going until I did it. You could take any from my list that resonate then carry on with your own. Keep that list to inspire and help you enjoy a relaxing day at home.

Day 23
Be financially chic

One subject I am passionate about is money. It is the cause of so much stress – and joy – in our life but really, it's only paper, metal and numbers. How is it that we make money a measure of our self-worth and how we feel about ourselves? How can we let it break up relationships, cause arguments or think that it would be the answer to our prayers if we won the lottery?

Money is a tool and, like other tools, we can use it to build a wonderful life for our family and to help others, or we can hurt ourselves if we don't pay it the respect it deserves.

If I had the power to revolutionise our school system, one subject that I'd make compulsory for all age groups would be the teaching of basic financial skills needed in everyday life. Along with maths, new entrants would be taught how to handle money and pay for goods in cash.

As students progressed through the school years, their financial education would be added to in an age-appropriate way so that children would leave school knowing about good versus bad debt, the importance of thinking early about their financial life and savings, compound interest, even touching on career choice as a means to building wealth.

It boggles me that we are taught very little about handling our finances; instead we learn a lot of number work including quite complex mathematical equations that, while good to know, are not as applicable in daily life.

Educate yourself

I spent most of my twenties working for financial planning companies and, while some of the administrative tasks were pretty dull, I learned a lot from listening to the advisers I worked with and also saw how life is better if you have sufficient funds to live without stress.

That period of my working life made me interested in finance and money; I read a ton of library books on the subject (there was no Internet in those days) and quickly found that while some were dry and filled with graphs, others had a more light-hearted approach which made the information much easier to absorb.

One of my bosses held financial seminars for women that I helped to run with her. She did the speaking; I was her assistant. I found it fascinating to see an audience of women with an age range spanning decades who wanted to learn how to empower themselves in their financial lives.

I heard sad stories of women who, when they were divorced or became widowed, suddenly had to learn about a whole new subject they'd never had to deal with before. One older lady didn't know why her cheques were bouncing because she still had plenty of cheques left in the book; this was tragically unnecessary because she'd never learnt about money.

There were inspiring stories too, such as the young woman who came into our office to discuss her fledgling investment portfolio. She mentioned that she was buying her first home, with flatmates to help pay the mortgage. At that stage I was renting; the concept of owning my own home seemed so grown up and far away that I still remember the jolt I received from having my mind opened to possibility.

From these experiences I decided to educate myself about money so I could emulate the success stories I had heard, rather than be one of the unfortunate cautionary tales.

Become debt-free as quick as you can

There are those, such as Robert Kiyosaki, who advise never being debt-free. He believes in leveraging yourself to become wealthy by always having 'good' debt, which means debt against income-producing or appreciating assets such as a business or rental property.

I am a more financially conservative person whose first goal is to be debt-free. I love to think of the freedom of paying no interest but collecting it instead. I was inspired by an old saying which said 'those who understand interest earn it; those who don't, pay it.' It has always stuck in my mind.

The first debt to focus on clearing is consumer debt ('bad' debt) such as credit card balances, car payments, overdue accounts and hire purchases. Many of us have made unwise financial decisions in the past (me included) and it can be a long time before we are free of the consequences of those decisions. If you consistently chip away at the balances without adding new debt, as much as these debts feel like mountains you will conquer them.

After eliminating consumer debt, the next step is to focus on your home loan or mortgage (or saving for a deposit on your first home and getting into one as soon as possible if you are renting). Because my husband and I have no consumer debt anymore, this is where we're up to and we are now on track to pay off our home loan early because we have been making extra payments. We decided to prioritise these extra payments over purchasing new gadgets and overseas holidays.

That's not to say we have not had a vacation since we bought our house, but we've definitely had less than we might have. In fact, we took our first overseas trip together a couple of Christmases ago – we called it our belated honeymoon because it was six years after getting married. We did not have a honeymoon at the time because money was tight; we took a mere one day off before returning to run our business.

Rather than feeling deprived, we now have a sense of excitement for the impending date when we will own our house outright – it's not long now. So how have we achieved this?

When we first bought our home, we had a twenty-five-year mortgage; I entered our balance into an online financial calculator (provided by our bank) then clicked on 'five years' to find out the repayments.

The repayments were quite a bit higher, but thrillingly we realised we might be able to manage the stretch, especially with such a tempting outcome. We decided to make those payments onto our mortgage, with the understanding of our bank that we could go back to the twenty-five-year plan if we found the increased payments too difficult to maintain.

Almost four years in and we've kept up the payments. Strangely enough, our lifestyle isn't so different and we don't feel like we've had to sacrifice much. We choose to cook at home most of the time, we wait for new technology and we share one car. We still have our treats and I feel like we have a good balance of saving and spending.

In a year's time, when we are mortgage-free we can

re-evaluate whether we want to move and upgrade our home or stay where we are, putting that extra money into investments.

Before we bought our home we were preparing for this. Our goal was to buy our own home so we wanted to build up a decent deposit. We were both on the same page and decided to throw everything at it. Instead of feeling pinched and frugal, it was a fun game to us and exciting too, because at the end we'd have our own home. I heard a slightly cheesy but fantastic saying which I adopted – 'teamwork makes the dream work'. It's true – you both have to be on the same team with the same goal. I'd say it out loud when either of us were feeling discouraged.

Here are a few of the ways in which we put money aside for our deposit; in fact, we still follow many of these practices today because they became habits. Then, in the future they will help our investment portfolio grow.

Make home a place you love to be

We enjoy each other's company and love spending time relaxing in our own space. Even when we were renting, we loved being at home because it was clean, comfortable and stylish so we hung out cooking, eating, talking, watching movies, reading and enjoying hobbies. *Make your home such a nice place to be that you'd prefer to spend time there than anywhere else.*

You can choose to eat at home instead of go to a restaurant, for example. You can have a carpet picnic if you feel like doing something different – push the coffee table out of the way then spread a blanket on the floor. We love to eat dinner on the sofa watching our favorite television programme or a movie. I don't care if it's not chic to eat in front of the television, we love it – our life, our rules!

Top up on inspiration regularly

I love to encourage myself on the topic of living well without spending pots of cash. There are many great books and blogs, which means you will easily find writers that resonate with you, whether you live by yourself in an apartment in the city or are a homesteading mother of four in the country.

Much inspiration is universal; immersing yourself in it means you'll feel like you're not on your own against the tide of consumerism and keeping up with the Joneses that goes on.

I do have a caveat though – my secret is that I only took in information if it made me feel good. If I felt poor or broke reading a savings tip I passed it by, because some tips are *really* penny-pinching and just make you feel bad.

For me, I prefer to focus on living simply and abundantly than on how much money I can save; we're all different though, so find out what makes you feel good and go with that.

Borrow your books first

If you love reading, consider joining the library. I used to buy every book I read which not only drained my bank account but I had *so many books* – my shelves were overflowing. I once offered them to a second-hand bookstore when I had a big cleanout and was shocked that recent books in perfect condition were offered only a fraction of their original cost (1/15th!). That was a great lesson for me.

Now if I want to read a book I borrow it from the library first if possible. After I've returned it, I can decide if I want it for my home library. I still have a lot of books but I love them all and reference them regularly.

Reconsider pay television

Not having pay television has saved us a lot of money. We've spent some of that on DVD rentals and purchasing DVDs, however I still believe we are well on the right side of the ledger.

This habit also taught us discernment in what we watched – we actively chose what we wanted to view, rather than let inertia dictate it. We recorded shows we wanted to view and had those to enjoy – we'd often wait until the end of a series then watch the season all in a row – it was like our own box-set, but free.

Even now that video-streaming subscriptions are inexpensive I'd probably not change my mind – I want to watch less television, not more – I don't need the temptation!

Luxuriate every once in a while

For us, it is important to have pockets of out-and-out luxury to keep up both our morale and the fun factor. Once or twice a year, we plan a trip to our favourite five-star hotel, spending the night there. We sit in the ornate French chairs being served cocktails and canapés, saying quietly to each other 'this is it, this is our life', imagining what it would be like to live in an apartment like the hotel suite we're staying in.

We are on their mailing list so when a special offer comes out we book a stay a few months ahead. Looking forward to it is half the fun – we even plan what we are going to wear to our evening drinks. It's like a mini-vacation without the travel costs or time off work.

Look at your regular outgoings

I read an interview with a self-made millionaire who said his cellphone coverage business had thrived on small regular income payments. Because the amounts were minimal, people happily paid each month, but all those small customers added up to big profits for his company. He said that for the same reason he disliked small regular payments going *out* of his bank account – they added up to big amounts over time – so he kept an eagle eye on his regular outgoings, reducing them where possible.

Some outgoings like rent or mortgage are necessary, others such as a gym membership are discretionary. I became extremely bored going to the gym so I was happy when my membership ended. I walk outside instead for free now and love it.

My husband however, loves his gym workouts, and it would take dire financial circumstances for him to give them up. He goes to a local gym near our business which means it's easy for him to get there and he rarely misses a session, usually working out five days a week. It's not a big fancy inner city gym and the price reflects that.

If you do belong to a big fancy gym, love attending and go all the time, fantastic, but if you belong and don't often go, reconsider that payment.

Another discretionary area I deleted was outsourced body maintenance. I used to have my legs waxed and manicures done regularly. That was easy to quit; I now shave my legs every few days and do my own nails once a week. Something I can't do myself is a massage, so every once in a while I'll book an appointment.

I have my hair cut and blow-waved every couple of months, but don't have it coloured currently. Sometimes I have subtle highlights (so subtle that there isn't an obvious regrowth), other times I don't colour at all. Now that my medium-blonde hair is turning silvery, I tell myself I am gaining platinum highlights that not even money can buy.

Rent or buy in an area that is not too expensive

It might not be your ideal place to live, but look at the decision long-term. You will be able to move up to a better suburb later on in a more effortless way if you make intelligent, strategic decisions now.

My father-in-law wisely said that if you have everything at once, you won't have anything to look forward to, so I remember that when I'm driving through a neighbourhood far ritzier than ours.

Make a few more meals at home

Getting into the habit of making meals at home is a huge saving and a lot healthier. We make our own work lunches mostly, treating ourselves to 'bought lunch' sushi once a week on a Friday.

We look forward to Sushi Friday whereas I remember I used to buy sushi five days a week – it cost me a lot and I didn't appreciate it nearly as much as I do now. It's the same with coffee – I don't have a bought coffee often, but when I do, I really enjoy it.

Eat out when it's for something special

Restaurant meals are mostly kept for special occasions such as our birthdays or wedding anniversary. Even inexpensive fast food or casual restaurant meals aren't 'cheap and cheerful'. Once we added up our costs for the evening, we realised we could have bought high-quality grocery items for the same price as an 'inexpensive' dinner out.

Knowing how to cook is a chic attribute. It doesn't have to take much effort or time – there are many simple and delicious recipes to be found. I often do an Internet search for a recipe and instead of searching for 'lasagne', for example, I will search for 'best quick and easy lasagne'. I'm all about smart shortcuts in the kitchen.

Be a slow adopter of new technology

A huge amount of money can be spent getting new gadgets when they first come out. If the most up-to-date technology is your thing and you have the money, go for it, but there are many people around who see their friends upgrading and want to as well, whether they need to or not.

I recently bought my first smartphone, and am finding the balance between being sensible with money and not falling behind on learning about new technology.

Use your nicest possessions

You are less likely to shop (or eat) mindlessly if you already feel surrounded by luxury; wearing your loveliest underthings and best clothes, spritzing your favourite perfume and eating from beautiful dishes.

Even if you are siphoning off most of your income to your mortgage account, you can still feel like an English Duchess luxuriating in your best finery. Most of us already have lovely items around our home that we could enjoy right now.

Choose your mindset to support you

Having a mindset of abundance, as well as being a respectful and good steward of your money is the perfect balance. It's all about prioritising what is important to you and funnily enough, if we became rich overnight, we'd probably be living much the same way as we do now.

I love to live a simple and beautiful life surrounded by my favourite people and comforts, enjoying ample time to indulge my creativity. Cruising the mall frittering away my money on cheap purchases or eating junk food doesn't go with that scenario so I am happy not to do them.

This wasn't always the case for me, I used to love nothing more than a trip to the mall to have a look around, buy a few trinkets and get something yummy to eat. I don't know how it changed; it must have happened gradually until I noticed one day it had been months since I'd stepped into a mall and when I did it was overwhelming – the lights were bright, it was noisy and echoey with children screaming, loud music coming from every store and tacky merchandise all over. It was such an assault on the senses that I try to avoid malls as much as possible now.

Being debt-free gives you freedom of choice

Having low levels of debt means we won't be as badly affected by a possible future financial downturn which keeps me feeling stress-free. A good investment is one that lets you sleep at night and security is huge for me.

Make a plan for your debts – list them in order of priority then work at eliminating them. By focusing on becoming debt-free, you won't be as tempted by new 'interest free' deals or sales promotions because you will be too excited by the prospect of being freed from consumer debt and your mortgage.

Keep your eye on what you want – being free and clear – not what you don't want (indebted). When you are wavering, have a mantra that you can repeat to yourself to get back on course – something like 'I love my freedom' or 'I'm on my way to becoming a millionaire!' Feel excited knowing that being financially secure *will* happen; once you get the ball rolling it could be sooner than you think.

When you are debt-free you have so many more choices about what you could do with your life. If we had a huge mortgage and continued to spend on credit cards, I would be trapped working five days a week. As it is, I'm thinking ahead a few years and it is a real possibility that I could work part-time, or even work from home as a writer, because we don't need that huge income to service our debt.

I do want to save for retirement, but I don't want to sacrifice my life now so if I can work part-time or from home in my forties and beyond, that would make me very happy.

What do you value?

For a long time now, I've opted out of what is considered 'normal'. I prefer to run my own race; what I value influences how I spend my money.

I value **security** so I am happy to make extra payments on our mortgage to be debt-free sooner (and not have purchased such an expensive home in the first place).

I value **knowledge and learning** so I am happy to invest in books and courses that interest me.

I value **health** so I invest in good quality foods and regular body maintenance appointments such as the dentist and doctor.

I don't care to 'keep up with the Joneses'. If I did, we would probably own a beach house and jet-ski, vacation overseas twice a year, have two brand new cars and live in a big home in an expensive neighbourhood. Of course, we would have the associated high-six-figure debt to pay for all of this as well.

None of these are bad in themselves however I value a low-cost, low-stress life more than I value those expensive items.

Choose what is important to you without being swayed by what others are doing.

Thirty Chic Days inspirational ideas:

If money scares you, commit to **finding out more** about it – there are many great money books and blogs to educate yourself with.

I love to read Amazon reviews of money books because often the reviews summarise the book for you, so not only do you get useful information straight away but you can then decide if it's a book you'd like to invest time and money in.

Some of my favourite books/authors to start with are:

The Millionaire Next Door and *Stop Acting Rich* by Thomas J. Stanley
Get Rich Lucky Bitch by Denise Duffield-Thomas
The Richest Man in Babylon by George S. Clason
The Automatic Millionaire by David Bach
How to be Wildly Wealthy Fast by Sandy Forster

Find blogs that resonate with you – do an Internet search for 'money blog' or 'personal finance blog'. You'll find some that spark excitement in you straight away. I have found out about new books, exciting challenges and been given great ideas and motivation from personal finance blogs.

If something in this chapter, in a book or on a blog gives you an idea to try, **implement it straight away**. You might set up an automatic savings amount or index fund investment. Even a small amount is worth doing because not only is it symbolic (you are ready to invest) but you have started your forward momentum.

A few years ago, even though we still had a mortgage, we started a $50 per month index fund investment. I love that it is ticking away behind the scenes adding to our future wealth – I already feel like a proper investor!

Be excited for your wonderful life where you are becoming more prosperous every day.

Day 24
Live a life of luxury

Even though I adore a quiet life and enjoy my daily routines immensely, *even though* I have a fabulous time cultivating simple pleasures and crave low-key-ness in everything I do, there is something about living a life of out-and-out-luxury that calls to me.

I like to imagine how blissful it would be to have the lifestyle of a millionaire where every whim is taken care of, where my household tasks are magically done and I fall to sleep at night with someone massaging my feet (I'd totally love that).

On the rare occasion that I'd purchase a lottery ticket, I would daydream about what the winnings would buy me. It was fun to get carried away with my rich girl millionaire list. The time before you find out you haven't won is almost worth the cost of the lottery ticket itself. It's a beautiful feeling of possibility.

I don't buy lottery tickets any more (I heard them called 'a tax on the poor' which put me off) but I do have a savings plan of $20 each month into a product here in New Zealand called Bonus Bonds. You don't receive any interest on that money, but you get a chance to win up to $1 million, twice a month. I thought that was a good compromise between buying lottery tickets and not, plus I still get to have my millionaire fantasy.

My dream 'millionaire lifestyle' list includes such luxuries as:

- Fresh flowers every week
- A daily housekeeper so that our home is beautifully kept
- Beautiful candles everywhere
- An elegantly styled home with high-quality furnishings
- Regular travel, both international and local
- Dining on fresh seasonal foods such as those that would be served at a spa resort or five-star restaurant
- A chef who makes us delicious meals three times a day so I'm not tempted by unhealthy foods
- Luxurious body maintenance on a regular schedule (exfoliation, self-tanning, manicures, pedicures, waxing, hairstyling, facials)
- Regular full-body massages
- Never thinking about the price of something – if I like/need/want it, I can buy it

- Plenty of time for reading, writing, thinking, dreaming, creating, planning and studying
- Time to potter in the garden
- Time for knitting, sewing and crochet
- Time for yoga, stretches, breathing and learning to practice simple meditation
- Being slim and healthy as well as looking fabulous in my high-quality, beautifully curated, minimal wardrobe
- Having long, silky hair that always look great
- Having down-time to *be*, with time to rest

Then I thought to myself, half of this list – more than half – I can have right now. The rest I can gain the *feeling* of, which is just as important.

For example, I might not have a daily housekeeper, but with a decluttered and tidy home that is quick to clean up, I can have that luxurious feeling of space, order and cleanliness right now. I might not have a chef, but I can feel inspired by a well-set-up kitchen.

It doesn't escape my notice that I crave unscheduled time, as well as time to do the things I enjoy. That simply involves prioritising and not wasting time on things that aren't important to me such as mindlessly browsing the Internet. I don't watch much television but I certainly have my fair share of screen time which I'd be willing to bet is only minimally enjoyable or productive. The rest could easily be done away with so that I'd have more time to spend doing the things I truly value.

I realised it all comes down to being intentional. On a rare, precious day off at home, I might feel like I want to be completely unstructured with my time, but the truth is that I'd feel unsatisfied at the end of the day if I am.

I decided instead to be unstructured within boundaries, which is similar to what I read about French parenting. Apparently French parents traditionally are quite strict with their children, but within those strict parameters they let their children choose. I like this idea and have found it works well with planning my day.

I then have more time for my crafts, to create, to read novels, to prepare luxuriously fresh foods and generally *be*. *That's* the dream life I'm talking about; thankfully I don't have to waste money on a lottery ticket to have it.

It's exciting to think that there is little stopping me from committing to living a life of luxury right now, instead of waiting for that magical unicorn-like day in the future. Reading through my dream list is so enticing that I want to start doing all those things immediately, no dilly dallying.

Use your luxurious belongings

Another aspect of living like I've won the lottery is that I won't use threadbare towels, chipped plates or anything broken or dirty. I've become pretty good at this over the years and when I do come across an area that has slipped between the cracks, I tidy it up.

A recent example of this was hiding in my wardrobe – my at-home lounge clothes. I know many people also have this issue because my post on *What to wear at home* is currently the most popular post of all time on my blog *How to be Chic*. I do try to look chic and stylish whilst still being comfortable and practical when at home in the evenings, but every so often standards can slip.

I'd already worked out my 'uniform' of leggings and a slouchy top (sometimes a clingy top with leggings when I'm feeling slim), but found myself with two pairs of leggings that both had small holes in the crotch. I know, not terribly chic at all. They were inexpensive to start with and not keeping their shape anymore, so it was time to invest in a new pair of leggings or two.

I also moved three designer tee-shirts that didn't feel quite right with my day clothes (they had large graphic prints on the front) to my loungewear drawer and they feel great for at-home or exercising. I do love a successful re-purpose, don't you?

Once upon a time I might have thought that the tee-shirts were 'too good' for lounge wear, continuing to wear them in public and not 'waste' them at home. These days I do what feels right *and* I feel special wearing such fancy tee-shirts just for me.

There are many other ways in which I use my luxurious items – spritzing on my Chanel perfume for work 'just because' (instead of saving for infrequent occasions that are deemed special enough), keeping only our three sets of white sheets and donating the rest (crisp white sheets make our bed feel hotel-like) and using my nana's English 'Belle Fiore' dishes regularly and with pleasure.

I don't need to go shopping to live a life of luxury because most of the things I could use are already to be found in my home. I'm willing to bet that if you go on a treasure hunt, you will also find plenty of 'kept for best' items you could start using more regularly. Instead of thinking 'what if they get broken, stained or used up?' focus on the enjoyment of their use. It's a far greater tragedy that they never see the light of day than be damaged during use.

Think of the beauty of a table set with crystal glasses and linen napkins for an everyday meal rather than plain glassware and paper towels. I donated a couple of shoeboxes full of glasses that I didn't particularly like (we had so many – they seem to breed in the cupboard) so we only have our nicer glasses now, as well as exclusively using cloth napkins at the dinner table.

This is a great way of enforcing using only your best– donate everything else, then you'll have no choice.

It's easy enough to do a hot soak wash for cloth napkins, dishcloths and tea towels once a week; if you flick them before hanging to dry (or fold straight away after the dryer is finished) you won't even need to iron them. They flatten down in the drawer too. I like to think of this look as 'vintage rumpled' instead of 'lazy tart'. I'm all about efficiency in creating a lovely life that is full of ease.

Choose your own state of luxury

What looks like a life of luxury to me, may not look like a life of luxury to you. We all have different ways in which we wish to live; what I have found is that true happiness comes from deciding what *you* want rather than following another person's formula. It's great to be inspired by others, but ultimately you will want to infuse into your life only those customs and possessions that truly make you happy.

For a long time I assumed a luxurious life consisted of expensive new cars, five-star hotels, super-fine clothing that needed dry cleaning and eating out at fancy restaurants.

When I wrote a list of what a luxury life meant to me, it was not those things, which felt like such a relief. I could live *my* luxury life, not the stereotypical one in a lifestyle magazine.

My luxury life is much simpler. I crave the luxury of free time to read, create, be, dream, watch movies and have luxuriously early nights. I love being financially secure and of always having that safe feeling of knowing I can pay the bills as well as save for the future. I never want too much on my plate so I'd rather have less to look after than more.

This is a definition of luxury that really appeals.

Thirty Chic Days inspirational ideas:

Take some time with your journal to ask yourself **'what feels luxurious to me?'** and 'what would my ideal lifestyle look like?' See if there is any way you can bring these things into your life either now or, with planning, in the future.

Include your spouse in these dreams and keep your family in the loop with your desires. That way it won't be such a big surprise to them when you announce 'we're leaving our jobs, renting our house out for a year and travelling around the world starting in South America'.

Friends of ours did that recently which made my husband and I think 'wow, how incredible – could we follow our dreams like they are?' then 'what *are* our dreams?'

Think about what you'd spend your lottery winnings on – don't hold back! It can be quite illuminating. Write a big list without pre-judging yourself. It's fun to read back through and you might find more inspiration for your ideal life. Even outlandish entries on your list can spark off great ideas.

As you go about your day, **notice areas where you're being cheap with yourself**. Are you using a ratty old hairbrush when you have a newer one already, or could replace it inexpensively? Are you using mismatched glassware (in a non-Shabby-Chic way) when you have a new set still in the box? Do you dress well when you go out but get about in rags at home?

Look at all these areas as a way to make incremental upgrades. It doesn't take much money or effort to start to **feel like a million dollars**.

Day 25
Collect contentment in petite measures

There is always so much happening around us that it's easy to feel swayed and discontented with our lives. We see friends and neighbours upgrade their cars, their patio furniture or their kitchens; come winter, you hear people talking about their tropical vacations and, even though you hadn't given any of these things a second thought, you now feel dissatisfied with your life.

Knowing that it is human nature to compare ourselves with others doesn't help us feel any better; even though we know this logically it *still* doesn't help because feelings are emotional so can sometimes be quite irrational.

How to feel content with your life exactly as it is right now

We recently visited friends who have a home that is newer than ours. The carpet is beautifully soft and pristine, their kitchen looks shiny and modern; when we arrived back home to our twenty-five-year-old abode, it seemed so dated by comparison.

Then I reminded myself of what I already know: we are only planning to live where we do for the next couple of years. For the sale price we would get for this home it's not worth the expenditure it would take to update. Everything is clean, functional and in good working order and we are making extra payments towards our mortgage because we are not putting money into renovations.

Our friends are in a different situation. They are planning to stay where they are for a while so they invested in a nicer home in a good school area. Remembering this was helpful in dissolving my discontentment in this situation.

Reclaim your power to feel happy with how you live and what surrounds you by focusing on your own life, not on other peoples. Changing your way of thinking helps you feel contented and grateful; it's a much nicer place to reside than in the murky neighbourhood of envy and dissatisfaction.

A better way to feel is to spark off excitement rather than discontent when seeing how others have done well for themselves. You can think 'I am happy where I am right now *and* I am excited to look to the future knowing that the best is yet to come. Good things are happening for me as well'.

How cultivating contentment can save you money

Good money decisions are *never* made when you're trying to keep up with the Joneses. Whether it's a show home you're visiting on a lazy Sunday, browsing fashion stores or perusing online shopping sites, remember the vision you have for your life.

I have a consistently beautiful dream where I crave a simple, uncluttered, low-cost life – these thoughts are the vision and inspiration I have for myself. Yet I also love the thrill of the chase so I find temptation in hunting down something online at the best price or browsing in pretty homeware stores. What stops me making too many impulse buys now is that I think past the purchase to bringing that item home (or having it delivered); the gloss often wears off before I have even paid for it.

What do I want with another perfumed body lotion, bottle of fragrance, scented candle or silky top? I already have too many – they are my repeat offenders! Conversely, the more of these items I have, the less content I feel. It's only when I make a concerted effort not to buy, instead using up all my beautiful toiletries that I feel a sense of peace and contentment – and abundance.

In the case of the show home, what I'm drawn to are the clean, tidy rooms with vacuumed carpets and a shiny kitchen sink. I need to get home and clean and tidy *our* house then I'll appreciate it as much as I covet that show home. Plus, it's a fun thing to look forward to the day when we *can* move into a nicer home (it's also a good incentive not to waste money on forgettable items that happened to catch my eye that day).

Cultivating contentment is a fabulous antidote to overspending – it saves you money and makes you happier. Win/win.

Why we are drawn to contented people

Whenever I spend time with someone who seems content with their life, themselves and what they've chosen to surround themselves with, I want to move *into* their life. Contentment is so appealing in an 'I'll have what she's having' kind of way.

It's only afterwards that I realise the only way to live *their* life is to be that person too but in *my* life. Be that person who has discernment in their choices and is genuinely happy with how their life is unfolding, like it's a customized plan or something – what a revelation!

It can be helpful to look at yourself as an outsider might, to see all the ways in which your life is wonderful right now. As for the actions that don't seem to fit into that life? Awareness is the first step and also a great place to start on aspects that don't fit your vision.

Thirty Chic Days inspirational ideas:

Here are a few of my favourite ways to sink back into contentment when I've had my head turned by comparison. See how many apply to you and note down any of your own that are sparked off by this list.

Gather gratitude for all that you have right now. Look inwards to your own world to see how magnificent it is as well as how much there is still to come. Look forward to your beautiful future with excitement and anticipation. If you choose to believe your life is a fabulous creation, it will be.

Be aware of the media you consume – glossy fashion magazines often leave me feeling 'less than', so I've decluttered them from my life. Reading one every so often helps confirm this decision. I've also had a news fast for a while now and am happier since I don't feel depressed at the awful stories I hear yet can do nothing about. It's true that if something big enough happens you will hear about it, so don't worry about being left out of current events. Have you ever heard the news called 'the bad news'? Isn't that the best, most accurate name? Good news just doesn't rate.

Take exquisite care of your life and all its possessions. Treat yourself as you would a loved family member.

Feel proud of what you've achieved thus far. Congratulate yourself on all your accomplishments no matter how small or how easily they came to you.

Focus on what makes you feel peaceful and content in your life. If you can't think of anything, simply ask yourself 'where do I feel particularly satisfied in my life at the moment?'

Keep your life feeling free by not overloading yourself with obligations and possessions. It's hard to feel content when you have too much on your plate. Do not feel guilty saying 'no'; French women are famous for having strong boundaries around this.

Learn to appreciate the beauty of something without needing to own it. When I first heard this idea many years ago it caused a huge mindset shift for me which has helped me enjoy a more minimal lifestyle with ease.

Have your own inspiration to read when you're feeling adrift. Mine ranges from printed-out posts from my favourite blogs to simple-living articles I've cut from magazines. You know the type – 'I moved from a corporate career in Manhattan to a cottage in Iowa where I spend my days knitting and making soup' – I love those stories!

Day 26
Make every day magical

If you have ever watched the movie *Amelie* starring Audrey Tautou, you may remember the way she appreciated her daily life. Amelie noticed all the tiny details around her, taking care with everyday routines such as bathing and eating.

Making a simple pasta dish was done in an unhurried way giving her dinner the due attention it deserved. She sat at a table simply but prettily set to eat her dinner for one – it was real food eaten from white ceramic dishes in a relaxed, dignified manner.

Of course the charm of Amelie and her quiet life wasn't hurt by the fact that she lived in a charming *bijou* (jewel-like, small and exquisite) apartment in Montmartre, a picturesque area of Paris.

I don't believe however, that living an Amelie-style life should be kept exclusively for those who live in

Paris or for those who have managed to perfect the classically French tousled hairstyle.

Don't make it all about one occasion

The more I live the European lifestyle of celebrating every day with good food, interacting with people in a respectful and friendly manner, and living my life with grace and passion; the more I realise this, *this* is the magical part of life. The special occasions are the icing on a deliciously rich, full-bodied cake.

Enjoying life every day is the motivating factor for me. Grand occasions come along so rarely that, if they are all we have to look forward to, we can be under the misapprehension that our life is routine and dull.

When we focus on something big such as a vacation, wedding or other special occasion, *willing* the days to go faster until we get there, we're missing out on all those other smaller but no less important minutes of our life.

Daily routines pass by on autopilot until the long-awaited time arrives when you will be married or start your vacation. Very soon it's all over and you are on the other side thinking 'now what?'

A work contact whom we saw regularly talked about her forthcoming wedding each time we met. She wasn't a bridezilla, but was *so* looking forward to her wedding. Her face was bright as she took us through the details and she seemed lit up by the upcoming day. The way she spoke, it almost seemed that she was more excited about the wedding than she was about actually getting married.

When we saw her again afterwards, she seemed quite down and this carried on for months. The day was gone and all she had were photos, memories... and a husband. She has moved jobs since then and I sometimes wonder how things are going for her (hopefully well).

Always have fun to look forward to

Along with daily happiness, to keep my life fun and exciting I like to have small- and medium-sized occasions to look forward to; in some ways I prefer to focus on them than the big events where I'm afraid for something to go wrong. I find there's simply less pressure on the smaller occasions.

Examples of little- and medium-sized plans I love are:

- Dinner out (or in) with family or friends
- A night at a fancy hotel
- An outing in the city, strolling, to have a look around and see what's new
- An evening at home with my darling and a DVD box set
- A movie night out
- My daily walks – I *love* my walks
- Using something new such as a scented candle I received for my birthday

- A planned shopping trip for something I need
- A massage or facial
- Cracking open a new novel – it doesn't even have to be 'new' new, I get excited about a new library book! It's the anticipatory feeling of launching myself into a fresh story that fills me with happiness
- Meeting up with a friend for coffee or lunch
- A day at home by myself to sew, knit or write – no housework necessary

Do little things that feel good every day

A big part of living a magical life is feeling good. When you go through the day with a low-grade sense of all those negative feelings such as guilt and not-enoughness, it brings you down which can lead to a loss of motivation and the thought of 'what's the point?'

To head off those thoughts, I compiled a list of all the little things that make me feel good. Every day I do as many of them as I can:

- Wear a sheer sweep of makeup and my favourite perfume on a day at home when no-one's going to see me. I love my perfumes so much that I often spritz more on throughout the day. It doesn't have to be the same one either – if it's good enough for Jo Malone to layer fragrances, it's good enough for me.
- Drink lots of water and an occasional herbal tea.

- Give myself permission to take a break and do something non-productive for a little while. I used to feel guilty about this and would create a false hunger to have a reason to stop; all this did was make me fatter which created more guilt. Now I can think 'I'm going to sit on my bed with the pillows stacked up and read for half an hour'. I tell you, this feels like the biggest bliss ever and I'm then happy to get back to my jobs.
- Not pack too much into a day and feel okay about not finishing my to-do list.
- Keep a creamy body lotion by the sofa to moisturise my hands and feet while I'm watching television.
- Sometimes stop and ask myself 'what do I want to do right now?', then do it. If you ask yourself and listen, you will hear the answer. If you don't hear anything straight away, keep asking and practicing.
- Lie on the floor for a big stretch, then lie there a bit more. It's less than five minutes but makes such a difference. I feel both rejuvenated and grounded. Usually one or both of my cats come to investigate as well, which I love.
- Wearing fabrics that feel good against my skin; often this means they are natural fibres, but they don't always have to be. There are many revolutionary fabrics around these days which feel (and look) incredible. I'm not a wasteful person but I have been known to get rid of an item of clothing if I don't like the texture of it and how it feels on my skin.

Make your life into a movie

Do your eyes glaze over when you turn the page to another magazine article espousing mindfulness? Me too. When I actually do it however, I'm amazed at how happy it makes me. Life seems to slow down while I notice all the details.

Sometimes when I'm watching a movie, all the little things shown such as walking through a leafy park or sipping a coffee with both hands wrapped around the warm mug seem so appealing. In my own life however, which is arguably more important than a fictitious movie, I rush through these moments with my mind a million miles away.

If I stopped to notice the colour of the leaves falling or took a moment to smell the gorgeous aroma of rich, freshly brewed coffee as I brought it to my lips, I could be living in a movie too – a movie of my life (cue the soundtrack).

Mindfulness slows you down. I seem to get so much more from my day and I'm simply blissfully happier. It's the days when I'm preoccupied that seem to whizz by, depositing me at the other end feeling frazzled with the house still a mess yet I've had no time for fun with my hobbies, reading or pottering.

From the time you rise in the morning until you fall asleep at night, notice what's around you. You don't have to do it all the time, but even doing it when you think of it will help slow down time, which in turn assists you in travelling through your day with ease.

You will also not end up with mysterious bruises all over you like I used to. I was rushing through my day literally bumping into pieces of furniture and doorframes because of the hurry *and not even noticing* that I was hurting myself. Does that sound chic and elegant to you?

Work through unfun tasks methodically

I love to take the time to make my daily routines as pleasant and beautiful as possible and to do my best when completing tasks. I find it easiest to manage this when I'm not rushing; even better, I now know that the rushed feeling was all in my mind.

I might say I'm busy with too much to do, but I know it's not the truth. The truth is I only need to rush when I've wasted time mucking around. When I go through my tasks in a leisurely manner, I actually enjoy doing them; even if it's something not that exciting such as washing the dishes or hanging clothes out on the line.

A bonus of this method is that I will often get everything done on my list and still have time left over for a leisure activity. At the end of the day I feel fulfilled and satisfied that my house is in order *and* I've had fun.

You may not expect, in a chapter entitled *Make every day magical* to find a section on paying the bills. They are a part of life though and my goal is to enjoy every day, even the days where I have seemingly boring tasks to undertake. I might not be able to make them magical, but I can try to make those tasks easier which in turn will leave more room in my day for other things, even if that 'other thing' is simply the satisfaction of completing a task I've been dreading for a while.

Tasks that I used to procrastinate on, even if they weren't that big, suddenly became easier to face when I said to myself at work 'right, I'm going to do the accounts filing every few days so the pile never gets too big' then did it with focus.

This works much better than my old method of putting it off until the last possible minute (when I had to pay them on the twentieth of the month). Each day I'd resentfully notice the growing pile while at the same time ignoring it, then – in a bad mood – rush through the accounts on the last day, getting grumpy if there was something I had to query 'because they have to be paid today!'

I did this most months without fail and I know my husband (we work together) did not look forward to this day because I made such a big deal out of it. So I changed the experience by the way I viewed it. I knew that I could expect a few invoices in my tray each day so I would file them every few days. If I noticed there was something to follow up, I'd have plenty of time to do so.

I'm certainly not perfect about it but I'm much improved, which makes me (as well as my co-worker/husband) very happy.

Be thankful for your good fortune

When I'm in a grump and gripy at my husband, a sure way to snap me out of it is to remember how incredibly fortunate I am. I begin right at the beginning of my life, in 1970, where I am thankful for the family I was born into. I love my parents and siblings *so much* and enjoy spending time with them too. We all have a lot of fun together.

I am thankful for being born in New Zealand. I love that we are quite isolated from the rest of the world and that I had a breezy and simple 1970s upbringing. I love that I was a teenager in the 1980s too – it was a fun fashion time where I felt free to wear puffball skirts and tease my hair.

I love that I was a child in pre-Internet times *and* I am grateful to be in that time now. I am grateful for learning so much from my 'starter marriage'. It has shaped me into the woman I am.

I am especially thankful for meeting the love of my life when I was thirty-two years old. I look forward to growing old with him, travelling to different countries together as well as enjoying our life at home.

I am grateful for all the pets I have known and loved. If you've ever had a pet, you'll know how good they are for your soul. I would not have laughed nearly as much if I'd never known my pets (all rescue animals – both cats and dogs).

There is so much in my life that I am thankful for; focusing on all the good makes it extremely easy to view my life as magical, *simply because it is*.

Thirty Chic Days inspirational ideas:

Compile a list of your favourite fun and luxurious activities, slotting a few into your calendar over the next few months. It doesn't even have to be for a special occasion. I don't have regular massages for example, but I adore them, so if it's been quite a while, I'll book one in.

Imagine your day as a movie. This is a fun thing to do. Starting when you get up, imagine you are acting in a movie – you're acting your most ideal self! There's an upbeat soundtrack playing (even if it's only in your mind) as you go about your day with ease, grace and style. Maybe an insouciant Audrey Hepburn is playing you or is it a sultry Monica Bellucci? Channel that thought.

Think of your worst task then work out a way to make it easy and fun, or at the very least easy. I often find that starting something is the biggest hurdle to get over. After I've done that, it's an easy downhill run.

List everything you love about your life – see if you can come up with one hundred. I bet you can. Say a big (but quietly spoken) 'thank you!' to the Universe.

Day 27
Embrace creativity and enjoy the benefits

When life becomes busy, it's my creative time that often seems to fall to the wayside. Hobbies that I love seem unimportant when I'm busy at work, and our home is messy and needs a good clean. Of course I want a peaceful home and a productive business, however I'm not doing myself any favours if I cast aside the activities that calm and relax me.

Conversely, when I make time for my creative pursuits, everything else seems to fall into place. There is suddenly time to knit, sew, read and potter, which is when I realise it's often unimportant time-wasters such as Internet browsing or excessive television watching that has spread into my craft time rather than actual useful tasks.

The satisfaction of creating with your hands

My favourite kind of hobby is where I end up with a handmade item. I haven't knitted a jersey (sweater) for a long time because they take me *an age* to finish by which time it's summer. Instead, I focus on knitting smaller pieces such as baby clothes and blankets, scarves, and home accessories like dishcloths and candle holder covers.

I'm excited to begin a new project and even more so once I've completed it. I like to give handmade baby gifts and have knitted five baby blankets over the past decade. Recently I finished a 'honeycomb' stitch infinity scarf (the 'Honey Cowl' from *ravelry.com*) in a beautiful deep red wine shade of pure wool (and it's actually called 'Merlot') which I look forward to wearing when it's cooler.

What if you aren't into crafts though? My aunty has said to me 'I'm not creative like you' when I show her something I've finished; yet she bakes weekly, entertains big family crowds with ease and has an amazing kitchen garden complete with exotic fruit trees. She also writes poetry and has done so for decades. Poetry, for goodness sake! I'd say she's pretty creative but cannot see it.

Creativity covers many areas such as playing a musical instrument, dancing, singing, acting, drawing, painting, crosswords and other puzzles (these call for creative thinking), quilting, patchwork, cooking, baking, cake decorating, art and music appreciation, origami, scrapbooking, writing, reading, making model airplanes (I actually did this as a teen!) and gardening to name but a few. It's not limited only to handcrafts and the list *is* actually endless.

You might not think you are creative, but maybe now you realise that you are.

What did you love to do as a child?

What did you delight in when you were a school-age child? Think about what you loved to play with and daydreamed about doing. It's different for each of us, but it's a great project to revisit what you used to enjoy when you were younger. For me, the list includes:

Crafts. I loved knitting and sewing when I was younger but I forgot all about them from my teen years until I was past thirty. When I revisited them, the happiness I felt then came back to me instantly. Now when I potter in my sewing room, I lose track of time and find myself feeling calmer.

Dolls. I have one living with me at the moment – my English *Mary Quant* 'Daisy' doll from the 1970s, along with all her clothes, both bought outfits and clothing I've made. I don't play with her often but it's nice to know she's there and I love to get her out when my nieces visit and put together pretty outfits with them.

Paper cut-out dolls. I don't have any cut-out dolls currently, but I used to love these and played with them right into my early teens. I graduated from the younger baby dolls up to fashion dolls with their more challenging outfits. Recently, when out shopping for a gift, I saw a Barbie activity book with fun star charts and a sticker cut-out doll. I was so drawn to it and it made me feel sparkling and happy. I resisted buying it for myself but maybe I should have!

Books. I have about a dozen books from my childhood, my favourites of course, which I adore having on my bookshelf. I browse through them sometimes and find them cheering to have around. I guess I've always been a reader because I love having my favourite 'comfort reading' on hand, both fiction and non-fiction.

Table tennis (ping pong). I was not that sporty as a girl, but loved to play table tennis if there was a table around. I even had my own bat. I think it is the only piece of sporting equipment I have ever owned... My husband has promised a ping pong table when we move to a bigger place. Hmmm, maybe we can have one where we are now, can't you get something that fits over your dining room table?

I found that creating this list made me feel happy and content because it brought back all the ways I used to have fun when I was young and life was simpler. It is also a fabulous list to refer to every now and then when I need inspiration because I realise I've become entirely too serious.

It will come as no surprise to you that I still love to read every day, play around with my wardrobe sorting and making new outfits, and knit and sew on a regular basis. I knit more than I sew at the moment but love that I still have my original sewing machine and overlocker (serger) from more than twenty years ago. I have plans to make my own Chanel-inspired capsule wardrobe of perfect pieces one day (and I know it will happen).

Another great idea to relax is to work on a jigsaw puzzle – they are so much fun and let you forget about real life for a while. They are satisfying to complete and you can go into a form of meditation as you hunt around for the pieces.

Did you know libraries loan them out? It's a great way to support your local library as well as keep clutter down. I often see them in charity stores too, so you could buy one to support that charity, then donate back when you are finished with it (which means there is no time limit as with a library item).

Hobbies are good for your mental health

There are many studies which show hobbies and craftwork can help those suffering from conditions such as chronic pain, grief, anxiety and depression. Engaging in something creative gets you into 'flow' where hours can pass like minutes because you are totally absorbed in what you are doing.

The brain is not able to focus on two thoughts at once, so it makes sense that by concentrating on a creative project your mind can calm down because it is not able to think about anything else at that time.

The outcome of being in flow is similar to that of meditation. I haven't yet had great luck in setting up a consistent meditation practice so that comes as good news to me. I can hand-sew patchwork pieces to create a beautiful cushion cover instead.

Hobbies are also great 'brain exercise' which can protect us from age-related ailments such as dementia and loss of cognitive function. Puzzles are a popular choice but if you're not a puzzle person, why not choose a hobby to keep your grey matter youthful.

Thirty Chic Days inspirational ideas:

Think of all the ways you are creative. You may overlook abilities that come easily to you – what do people often compliment you on? That's a good place to start.

Make a list of all the hobbies and interests that you enjoyed in childhood or that you'd like to try now. Don't filter as you write the list or think to yourself 'I'll never do that'. Freeflow and write down everything – don't stop until you get to twenty ideas. Some surprising thoughts may come through.

Read back through your list and **infuse yourself with the feeling of that hobby**. Notice how you feel: relaxed, happy, youthful, carefree? I promise that you will be keen to start with one of the items on your list. Have fun with it!

If you are going through **a particularly difficult time**, is there a hobby you can take up, maybe something you've never tried before? It might be the last thing you feel like doing, yet it could also be the perfect time-out for your stressed mind. Baking a cake or visiting a needlecraft store to pick up a small project may be the ticket to help you through.

Day 28

Think of your home as if it were a boutique hotel

As much as I wish I was one of those people who naturally loves to clean, I'm not. I've heard of mythical creatures who say they're happiest pottering about with rubber gloves and a bottle of Spray'n'wipe and, if it wasn't for my nana, I would say they were made up.

Whenever my nana visited, she would not be able to sit still and relax. She'd be out on our patio with a broom, sweeping away the dust and leaves. She couldn't visit either of her two daughters without getting out the vacuum cleaner, and was famous for the swish marks on her own carpet from her vigorous vacuuming style. Of course her compact and sunny flat was immaculately kept and clutter-free.

Sadly, this gene did not pass onto me, so I do the best with what I have. I've been through all the tips and tricks and am pleased to share those that I have found work well, assisting in my quest to have a home that is neat, tidy and clean most of the time.

This allows me the space to relax, create and share, free of the guilt and shame that often accompanies a home that is dirty and messy.

Inspire yourself

One thing that is nearly always guaranteed to make me feel more motivated and positive is to approach caring for my home as if it were a boutique hotel. And the guests? My family and I.

The Boutique Hotel technique. Imagine if you were going away for a long weekend somewhere. What kind of place would you choose to stay at? Would it be a country house with huge old trees, tartan carpets, plush sofas and a roaring fire? Or would it be a sleek inner-city hotel with silver pendant lighting and white walls? Perhaps a cosy country-style bed and breakfast? Or what about a funky industrial French chic boutique hotel, with zinc stools at the breakfast bar and polished concrete floors.

Thinking about all these places and how gorgeous they would be inspires me to clean, tidy and beautify my own home. It may not be as 'designer' as my imaginary boutique hotels, but I can make it as welcoming and stylish. I imagine my home as a lovely place to stay; a tranquil sanctuary and oasis of calm.

Approaching housekeeping from this angle makes whipping around doing the cleaning a breeze. While I'm working through my tasks, I can think of finishing touches I'd like to make.

Once I have completed the basics – changing the bed, cleaning the bathrooms and kitchen, vacuuming, mopping and dusting – and doing a little light decluttering – I'll light scented candles, rotate the few accessories I have out and sometimes even move our furniture around to make everything seem new.

I also have other techniques to alternate, so I never become bored. May I present to you...

The YouTube technique. I love to watch a short YouTube video to get me started. Like my nana, there are other people who love to clean, and, generously they have created their own YouTube channels to help us out. *How Jen Does It* is a great one and I love *VasseurBeauty* too; she's so much fun. Search around until you find someone who resonates with you. Simply searching for 'housework inspiration' or 'cleaning motivation' on YouTube or Google brings up fabulous links.

The Flylady technique. Flylady can be overwhelming because she has a lot of information, but usually only ten minutes on her Web site *flylady.net* helps me find something to give me the starting point I need.

The Perfect Housewife technique. I ordered Anthea Turner's *Perfect Housewife* television series on DVD from Amazon UK years ago and have almost worn the discs out from use. I'm sure there are US equivalents of this kind of programme too. Anthea visits hopeless housewives to sort them out with tough love. They declutter and clean their homes and I never finish an episode without finding myself raring to clean and tidy *my* home. If I need an extra boost, I imagine what Anthea might say if she walked in through my front door.

The Magazine technique. Imagine you are having a photo shoot done in your home for an interiors magazine. You might whizz around the whole house to clean but then focus on one room such as the living room or master bedroom to 'stage'. This makes housework fun and I love the results – it feels like a room on a magazine page afterwards. Take digital photos along the way to see how you're going. A photo picks up more than the eye; by viewing your home this way you'll find areas to tweak to make your room more beautiful. Through a photo you see things as another person might – with fresh eyes.

The Timer technique. I can easily let a few household tasks take me half a day (or even the entire day) if I'm not careful. Because housework is not my favourite thing to do I procrastinate about starting, take frequent breaks and do other more fun jobs in between. If I only have one hour to whip around our house, or don't want my housekeeping chores to take all day, I'll say to myself 'let's see how much I can get done in X amount of time or by X o'clock'. I then set off like an extremely efficient cleaning demon. My mind magically sorts through what the first priority is; I complete that, then move onto the second priority. The timer technique focuses my mind like nothing else.

The iPod technique. An audiobook or podcast playlist on my iPod is my current favourite way to happily potter around doing my tasks. I get through hours of interesting audio this way and I don't begrudge – or even notice – the time spent cleaning.

Tidy as you go

Another winning strategy to keep our house in order is to be diligent in putting items away as I go, as well as doing little jobs often. If something takes less than five minutes to deal with, I'll do it straight away.

Leaving one item on a table because I can't be bothered thinking of what to do with it is not a good plan. It could be as innocent as a takeout menu or a piece of junk mail, but before long it's joined by all of its friends who are magically attracted to it, so I end up with a dining table that looks cluttered and messy.

You have a much better chance of having clear and serene surfaces if you don't let objects settle. Either file the takeout menu in a drawer or folder if you plan to use it again, or recycle it if you don't. Read (or don't read) the junk mail then recycle that too.

It's so easy to put something down to deal with 'later', I've done this myself many times. However, it's just as easy to get into the habit of doing small jobs immediately. If something will take you only five minutes, do it straight away and see the difference it makes.

I have regular times of the day when I do a quick tidy and put things back as they were. I find the best times to be in the morning before we leave for work and after dinner before we go to bed. The kitchen is cleaned up, the dining and living areas where we've spent the evening are straightened up, then when we get up in the morning it's a nice start to the day.

Likewise, when we return from work, it's pleasant to be greeted with a tidy and clean living area as well as a peaceful bedroom with a neatly made bed. Making your bed pays such dividends in return for the five minutes it takes, as it pulls the whole room together. The rare time I leave the house with an unmade bed, it's horrible to come home to, rather demoralising in fact!

Plan ahead

Let organisation set you free by setting up your home for ease and comfort. To prevent chores from building up into a once-a-week all-day marathon, I try to do one small job most days. This helps my week run smoother so I'm less likely to feel overwhelmed and grumpy.

I used to think that this old-timey philosophy wouldn't apply to me because I work full-time. How could I do 'floors on Monday, laundry on Tuesday' etc. if I was at work both those days? But I found that if one job doesn't take too long, often only half an hour, I can do it while dinner cooks or maybe after dinner depending on what kind of mood I'm in or how tired I am. If I'm organised I can quickly finish a job before we leave for work.

This way on my days off I can complete a few chores, then relax with a long stretch of writing time or my hobbies. I love to have a clean and welcoming home, but if I spend both my days off achieving this I can quickly feel like I don't have a life.

I bought myself a Kikki K weekly goals planner pad where I note down jobs for each day alongside other goals such as exercise planned, writing projects I want to work on as well as personal development study. These are the sorts of things I love doing because they make such a difference to my life, but that can easily be pushed aside.

You could also do this in a diary or daily planner – space out housekeeping jobs throughout the week (or the month for less frequent tasks) so that everything is done with ease.

Invest in lovely cleaning products

In the past I've purchased supermarket cleaning products which were often unattractively packaged in garish colours with strong, fake scents. Then I changed to simple, natural cleaning products such as baking soda and vinegar. I don't use baking soda so much now, but I still use white vinegar all the time – I refill the window/mirror cleaning spray bottle with equal quantities of white vinegar and water which works perfectly. I use undiluted vinegar in a spray bottle to clean the toilet (it deodorises and has anti-bacterial properties).

It wasn't until I purchased a few prettily-scented upscale cleaning items to mix in with my natural products that I felt inspired to clean my home more often though, because my fragrant products are such a delight to use. I've tried brands such as Mrs Meyers and Method and I know there are many others. I love the scents of the Mrs Meyers products I have: Honeysuckle, Lavender and Geranium – the house smells wonderful when I've used them.

Essential oils, too, make a big difference. I clean our lino floors with half a cup of white vinegar in half a bucket of hot water; by adding several drops of an essential oil I can make it a more enjoyable experience – as much as it can be anyway.

I've even had a try at making my own Spray'n'wipe product which is pretty easy. There are many different recipes all over the Internet, but two I have had success with are:

All-Purpose Spray'n'wipe Recipe

In a 500ml (16 oz./1 pint/2 cups) spray bottle mix:
1 tablespoon baking soda
2 drops dishwashing liquid
10 drops tea tree oil
2 tablespoons white vinegar
Top up with water

Shake each time you use it and use as you would normally use a spray and wipe product.

Anti-Bacterial Bathroom Spray'n'wipe Recipe

In a 500ml (16 oz./1 pint/2 cups) spray bottle mix:
1 cup white vinegar
Juice of one lemon
Top up with water

Shake to mix and use as you would normally use a spray and wipe product. The vinegar and lemon juice kill bacteria.

If you don't have the different ingredients for these recipes, at least buy yourself a large bottle of white vinegar and use neat, or diluted 50/50 with water in a spray bottle as I mention above. Don't be too concerned about the vinegar smell; it dissipates within minutes; by then everything will simply smell lovely and fresh.

Don't be perfect

Perfectionism is something that has kept me from getting on top of my housekeeping more times than I care to remember. For example, if I have mending to do or there is a cluttery corner or my bathroom is looking messy, my mind goes like this:

'There's that mending to do but it's only one piece and other jobs that need doing are more urgent. Besides, I'd need to take my time over it'. *walk away doing nothing, mending is still undone*

'That corner is so stressy and I'd love to get into it and thoroughly declutter but I don't have time to do it properly. I'll do it another day when I can spare more time'. *walk away doing nothing, corner is still cluttery*

'The bathroom has toothpaste spatters on the mirror and the sink needs a wipedown. I can't do the whole bathroom today though so I'll wait until Tuesday which is my usual day'. You can probably guess that I *walk away doing nothing, mirror still has spatters*

In all these situations I expend tiny energy leaks each time I notice these tasks and don't do anything about them, and it all comes down to perfectionism. Perfectionism dictates that I can't do a partial job because obviously it's a rule that I have to do everything all at once and... perfectly.

Recovering perfectionists, can you relate to this? Perfectionism seems to be best mates with all-or-nothing, because I end up doing one of those two. The perfectionist part of me spends all day exhausting myself on a housework marathon, then wonders why I dread doing it.

Learning to be happy with 'good enough' is what stops me disappearing into the procrastination hole of my own perfectionist tendencies. Being okay with a home that is tidy and clean but not 'perfect' and not waiting for a time when I can 'do a perfect job' is a way in which I can help myself live a balanced life.

I am now happy to tidy up an area as it bothers me in between times, as well as do the best with the time and energy I have on my scheduled cleaning days. I do a good-enough job, and I don't exhaust myself.

Thirty Chic Days inspirational ideas:

If getting motivated is an issue for you like it is for me, **create your own housework inspiration**. Find a couple of sources of inspiration that resonate with you and which you can rely on to spur you into action, then keep them close to hand.

Do little jobs and **pick up items as you notice them**. It may seem bothersome at the time but you will notice a huge difference in the overall look of your home and also in your energy levels.

Space your jobs out into appropriate groups to see if it works better for you to do them over various weekdays. I mix this around – sometimes I follow the space-them-out method, other times it feels like I have a job every single day so prefer to do my jobs all at once for the week. It works for me not to be too rigid about it.

Consolidate your cleaning products to assess how much you like them and whether they do a good job. Use this time to declutter your stash if you have a tendency to go for the next wonder product before you've finished the last bottle. Commit to using something up before you buy another one. When you do need an item, try making your own or give yourself permission to buy something lovely for a few extra dollars.

Be happy with good enough. Perfectionism is linked with low self-esteem, so appreciating both yourself and your home as they are will help ease its grip.

Thanking the Universe for my home, my health and my life makes me so grateful to have all that I do. If I'm feeling dissatisfied with our abode, I walk around noticing all the good points about it and remember how excited I was when we first moved in. Doing this takes me back to a time when I was *thrilled* to live in this home and it helps shift my focus.

Day 29
Walk your errands

You might have noticed how 'naturally' slim people seem to walk everywhere, often having no trouble walking for miles. These people have a certain looseness in the way they carry themselves and seem comfortable in their own bodies.

This ease comes from the benefits of being more physical – not in a planned-exercise way, but in a many-small-moments-a-day way. They seem happier and healthier because they are honouring their natural state as human beings. The physical body wants to move freely, not sit hunched over a desk or steering wheel for hours at a time.

We might not be able to quit our office job and our commute to achieve this, but we can create other ways of adding movement into our day fairly easily; the most obvious one is the errand walk.

Join the slow-living movement

Walking errands in your neighbourhood feels good because it imparts a sense of connectedness and wellbeing. You interact with those you pass; it could be a smile or 'good afternoon' or (from me) 'your little dog is so adorable'. You take in the air as you stroll and feel like you're part of the world.

I have made a concerted effort to become more like my ideal French girl by walking many of my errands and it is now second nature to me. I look forward to these strolls and prefer them to jumping in the car. When I first started it felt like a big production where I had to allow a lot of time and be very organised, but now it's what I do more often than not.

Walking errands makes me feel quite European and like I am living the slower-paced French-fantasy life I've visualised for myself. It's quite thrilling when you realise you are putting into practice – effortlessly – what you've always dreamt about.

Be slimmer without changing anything else

Isn't it true that we magically seem to lose weight when on vacation, despite all that rich food and extra eating? Could the hours a day we spend sightseeing on foot have anything to do with it?

My mother recently travelled to Europe where she spent two nights in Paris with family members, one of whom had a pedometer app on his smartphone. At the end of their first Parisian sightseeing day he announced they had all walked 24,000 steps or sixteen kilometres (ten miles)! That is a lot of walking. No wonder we lose weight on vacation even though we're not restricting our food, eating anything we want.

We then arrive home, jump straight back into our car and it can be days – or even weeks – before we walk any further than from our car to the front door. We're surprised that our vacation weight loss rebounds so quickly, but perhaps we shouldn't be.

I've done this and found that the expensive designer jeans I bought in Rome did not fit me less than a month after I arrived home. That was quite depressing – not only had I become fatter but I'd completely wasted the money spent on my European denim *and* I had no new jeans to enjoy.

My goal is to keep my weight consistent so that I don't 'grow out of' my clothes; keeping active daily can assist with this, plus, choosing to walk errands is convenient for a formal-exercise-avoider like me. Deciding to start an ambitious exercise plan involves money, time, new clothes and lots of energy; deciding to walk a bit more each day does not. It feels easy and pleasurable.

Find errands you can switch to walking

There are many errands you can choose to walk instead of drive. For example, if you live close to the grocery store you could shop regularly on foot rather than drive there for a once-a-week jumbo shop. Knowing you have to carry everything home makes you choosier about what you buy. I don't want everyone to see my giant bulging supermarket bags carrying the 4/$5 potato chip special so I don't purchase them. A double win!

If you don't fancy carrying grocery bags home, you might have noticed it has become quite fashionable to pull a shopping cart. It's not only old ladies who do this anymore; it's more 'French market'. There are stylish, good quality carts available in bright colours, cute prints or simple and chic black. If you had something like that, you might feel more inclined to walk to do your grocery shopping. I haven't bought one yet, but then I don't mind carrying a few grocery bags.

We have a small shopping centre nearby which includes an English-style pub. In the summer it's nice to stroll there for dinner then walk home afterwards, it helps that it takes only eight minutes on foot each way. A gentle amble after dinner feels quite European and also helps digest the meal.

Our doctor's office is not far from where we live either, so I'll make an appointment on a day when I'm at home so I can walk there. It's the same with my hairdresser. I'd been going to one in the city and it was fine, but it was a hassle to get there. I tried one within walking distance from home where I found the young woman personable as well as doing a great job. Now I make an appointment every six weeks or so and enjoy the walk there and back. Not driving somewhere does wonders for your serenity.

Make it easy to choose walking

Deciding to walk more of your errands involves removing barriers. If there is somewhere you could walk to but never do, ask yourself 'why not?', taking note of the answers. Then you can address those excuses, sorry, reasons.

One of my excuses was that it might rain. I already had a fold-up umbrella which was small and light to carry, but I also invested in a nice lightweight rain jacket which looks like a short black trench-coat (I also mention this in '*Day 7. Honour your body with chic movement*'). It is Gore-Tex lined and has a hood that rolls into the collar. I've worn it almost daily over the winter months. It looks stylish with my everyday clothing and is perfect to wear on my exercise walks.

I saw someone else wearing the same jacket recently; before I realised it was *exactly* the same as mine I was thinking how nice she looked. I was so happy when I made the connection realising I had the same jacket!

Is one of your reasons that you don't have enough time? This is a slightly tougher one to address because it involves prioritising yourself, and possibly putting other people out.

Instead of staying at your desk during your lunch break, eating while reading a magazine but being there in case anyone needs you, leave at 1pm and have an errand planned for each day, even if your 'errand' is simply a twenty-minute walk.

You can take your lunch with you to eat outdoors in fine weather. There are many little seats or parks in city areas. It's also much better for you to get natural light and air during the day than spending a long stretch of time in air-conditioning with artificial light.

If I am at work and automatically think 'it will be quicker to drive to the Post Office than walk', I check myself then reframe it – 'nothing bad will happen if I'm gone for half-an-hour longer and it is honouring my health plus I will enjoy the stroll'. Sometimes I don't have enough time so I drive, but mostly I do and it feels self-loving to put my health and wellbeing first.

It's so enjoyable to be outside walking whether I'm in the city or the suburbs. I always feel chic and European when I walk to the post office or bank, or to pick up a library book, especially since I don't wear actual walking gear and I'm strolling in my normal clothes with comfortable shoes.

Walking places eventually becomes part of your normal life

You will find that you start walking further each time, walking to areas you would never have considered not taking the car. I routinely walk to both a nearby suburb and also the city for combined walks/browsing or any errands I might need to carry out.

If I happen to mention to a friend or family member I have walked somewhere, they are often aghast at 'how far' I have walked. Most places I walk to are only fifteen to thirty minutes each way. Okay, so you won't do it for a quick trip when you're short on time, but by walking there you are getting in exercise, dropping off a bank deposit envelope and checking out the latest fashions. Sounds good to me.

Grab your sunglasses, put on some lipstick and walk to pick up your vegetables for dinner tonight, just as your ideal French girl might. Even though you are unlikely to be strolling the streets of Paris, you can imagine you are. It's almost the same!

Thirty Chic Days inspirational ideas:

Make a list of errands you can convert from a car journey to a walk. Take into consideration not only the length of time it will take you to get there and back, but also what you might need to carry. It's not ideal to lug heavy bags so choose errands where there won't be too much to transport.

Think about any purchases that would **make walking errands enjoyable** – a good start would be a pretty and practical rain-jacket along with shoes that are supportive and comfortable, which go well with your everyday style.

If it's relatively close by, **walk to meet a friend** rather than drive. I met two colleagues for lunch one day, walking to meet them. It was the next suburb over which took about 45-50 minutes each way, but it meant I didn't have to find a park and I gained exercise and fresh air at the same time. It was a city suburb, so the people-watching was just an added bonus!

Day 30
Immerse yourself in sensuous beauty

Is there anything more delicious than the feeling on your skin when you pull on a soft cotton tee-shirt, breathe in the aroma of fresh coffee when walking past a café or the sight of a beautiful bouquet of flowers? All too often these moments are not noticed because we're busy rushing to get to the next thing.

Slowing down and appreciating all our senses on a daily basis will lead us further into the beauty and mystery of life. Easier said than done though, don't you think? So how can we practise this and what does it mean to live in a sensuous manner? Or to put it another way:

How can we feel sensuous on a daily basis without breaking the bank (or it taking so much effort that we don't want to bother)?

It's fine to be all ethereal and wafty sometimes, but I like to create concrete ideas; to dream up many different ways I can invite all of my senses into everyday life. This was a fun process and I tried to step away from clichés and find what truly spoke to me.

The sense of sight

- Lighting candles at home, whether we're watching a movie at night or I'm working on my laptop during the day. It's soothing and feels luxurious to have a candle flickering (even in the summer it's a nice touch).
- Taking twenty minutes to blow-dry my hair – in sections using a clip and a big round brush, like the hairdresser does. It feels and looks a million times better afterwards and all it costs me is a little time – and effort. It lasts for two or three days as well, so it's an investment in time worth spending. The added bonus is that the more I do it, the better and quicker I get at it too.
- Applying my makeup using a light hand, blending flawlessly thereby producing a glowing complexion and seemingly polished skin. I recently bought myself a foundation brush and love its professional quick results.
- Cutting flowers and foliage from the garden to create my own petite florist-worthy display. Our garden is not Versailles but there is always something to find if I look. I have a couple of larger

vases but prefer to use bud vases – a few flowers and pieces of fern looks so lush and impressive in a bud vase. At the moment they aren't particularly in vogue so I've picked up lovely ones from charity stores ranging from 30c to $1. Thrifty *and* chic.

- Enjoying a room that is light and airy with no clutter because I've done a quick pick-up and tidy. It's funny that sometimes I don't do this because I'm feeling lazy and unmotivated, but if I make the (what feels like) monumental effort to do so, I gain energy and motivation. Like most things in life, the effort comes *before* the result.
- Taking the scenic route when I go for a walk, even if it's only up the road on an errand.
- Liking how I look in the mirror because I've been working on my nostalgia/childhood food issues (eating kiddie treat food is *not* cute and endearing, I tell myself). Remembering the mantra 'I am enough' helps with this enormously.
- Being happy with my wardrobe because I've kept top of mind that I love simplicity of dress with classic lines and *don't* covet something trendy and new that I know from experience I won't wear beyond the first week.
- Rewatching a favourite movie that I know will inspire me every time – *The Devil Wears Prada*, Woody Allen films, *A View from The Top*, *Sweet Home Alabama* – yes, often they are very fluffy.

- Going to one of our public parks with a book and a rug, pretending that I am relaxing at a park in Paris – big sunglasses mandatory!

The sense of sound

- Choosing silence when I'm at home by myself instead of having something playing; drinking in the peacefulness – relishing it in fact. Any noise in the background such as the washing machine or a neighbour mowing their lawn becomes a calming domestic backdrop.
- Shopping where the sounds are soothing i.e. small stores rather than choosing to go to the mall, where loud clashing music and excited children's screeches echo around. Even better, I shop from home on my computer and have it delivered.
- Absorbing that très cool feeling when I play classic jazz and blues from favourites such as Miles Davis, Sarah Vaughan, Nina Simone and Dave Brubeck. How incredible is the invention of music that the same notes produce millions of different results that can impact how we feel within minutes?
- Feeling extremely elegant when I listen to the rich, refined sound of a violin concerto. I don't know many classical pieces by name, but I've loved Bach's Brandenburg Concertos for many years, so if you are a beginner pick this up on CD. You'll find it on YouTube too.

- The great summer sound of cicadas singing at night – I can't create this one for myself but I can look forward to it each year (and pretend I live in the South of France – the cicada is Provence's official symbol).
- Loving when it rains hard and I'm at home all cosy. Rain on the roof is one of the best sounds ever and even better if I'm nodding off to sleep. Pottering around my house or reading on the sofa with the rain lashing outside is a close second. I can't create this sound either but I can certainly fully appreciate it when we do have rain.
- Going to the beach and soaking in the sounds of waves crashing and seagulls squawking. Instant vacation feeling.
- Recognising someone's voice and receiving an involuntary feeling of love for them.
- Turning my attention to my *own* voice – is it nice to listen to? Could I speak slower, deeper, softer, not so often? Speak nicer words and swallow the harsh ones?
- Hearing someone with an uncontrollable and quite comical laugh – it sets off your own even though you haven't heard what made them laugh and sometimes it might be a complete stranger that makes you laugh from their contagious laugh. Along the same lines, finding something funny – a short YouTube video perhaps – to flood your body with feel-good endorphins. I love to look up Harry

Enfield, Amy Schumer, Sebastian Maniscalco among other comedians.

The sense of touch/feel

- Choosing soft fabrics that feel great against my skin. Donating clothing that I don't like the texture of (there are clothing items I subconsciously avoid because I don't particularly enjoy the feeling of the fabric they are made with).
- Being surrounded by water in a swimming pool or the sea – under the sun, floating on my back.
- A brisk walk with the wonderful feel-good effects afterwards.
- Smooth, moisturised skin – I love collecting pretty body lotions and creams to use many times a day. I always do my full body after a shower – yes, there is time!
- Giving myself a pedicure and smoothing my heels with an exfoliating paddle, then moisturising with a rich body butter afterwards. Clean, fluffy house-socks help my feet feel cosseted and the moisturiser soak in. Absolute bliss.
- Holding my darling's hand to feel safe and loved.
- Stroking our cats' soft fur and, when we had our dear elderly rescue poodle, I used to love the feeling of the little ringlet coat he grew – so unique to poodles.
- Hugging family members tight when they're coming or going.

- Opening windows at home whether it's warm or cool, so that I can feel a breeze or at least the movement of air through the rooms. Even (or especially) rooms that aren't used as much – it's nice to have fresh air circulating.
- Having an afternoon shower, which to me always feels like I'm on vacation, whether I am or not.
- Saying (or thinking) words to myself and soaking in the feeling they evoke: words such as refinement, softness, elegance. Peace, ease, calm, serenity. Tranquility, love, aah, there are so many words that make me feel happy and content.

The sense of smell

- Choosing body products with beautiful scents – 'fragrance free' is not a selling point to me, I adore all those pretty fragrances. I love using Elnett hairspray because it has such a feminine, luxurious scent reminiscent of Chanel No. 5.
- Clean washing hung on the line – damp and fresh; then full of the smell of sunlight once it's dry.
- Having different genres of perfume so I can choose how to feel for the day – fresh, bright and youthful, sultry and sophisticated, ready to take on the world; it's all there, any type of feeling I wish to evoke.
- Enjoying food aromas such as freshly brewed coffee, bread baking, bacon sizzling, or a buttery, oaky Chardonnay. It's not even necessary to eat or

drink an item in order to enjoy the aroma. When I was a teen, I had a school holiday job at my cousin's store in a tiny and lovely mall. There was a boutique chocolatier nearby and I can still remember the exquisite bouquet of rich chocolateyness as I walked past the store each day.

- Going for an early walk to breathe in fresh, damp, morning air.
- Catching a fragrant wisp of woodsmoke on a winter's evening – also the enticing smells of neighbours' dinner cooking when we arrive home hungry after work.
- The spring smell of freshly cut grass – I know it's a cliché but it's a cliché for good reason – it's one of those smells that makes you happy to be alive. Plus, it means the sun is shining which is always a good thing.
- Stepping inside a florist's shop – there are no other words for this than *simply divine*. All those different flowers, all at their peak of freshness.
- Enjoying the earthy smell of the forest – trees, bark, leaves – even simply thinking about it I can conjure up a peaty aroma.
- Describing bouquets of different wine varietals. I don't drink, but my husband is a wine enthusiast and I've learnt so much from him. I'm getting pretty good at picking the type of wine by sniff only. I also come up with some excellent descriptions (if I don't say so myself) – it's fun to be a non-drinking wine buff.

The sense of taste
(without taking in too many calories!)

- The refreshing mouthfeel of chilled, sparkling mineral water (served in a champagne flute, always).
- Ripe seasonal fruit at breakfast. From this change in my diet I've learnt so much about which fruits are in season and when.
- Water-rich fresh, raw, salad vegetables with lunch. So refreshing and thirst-quenching: the tanginess of a garden tomato, sweet lettuce torn into pieces, capsicums (bell peppers) for a different texture and flavour.
- Gourmet fish and chips, my favourite takeout meal. Calorific yes, but we have it so infrequently that I don't worry about this too much. When we do partake, I enjoy it fully. My husband taught me that if you're going to have something you may as well enjoy it; don't wreck the experience with guilt.
- Petite amounts of rich foods such as double-cream brie, organic half-and-half and 90% cacao chocolate.
- Oysters eaten raw with lemon juice squeezed over – not to everyone's taste but I love them.
- Freshly made salmon and avocado sushi for lunch (our Friday treat).
- A steaming hot cup of Earl Grey or English breakfast tea first thing in the morning; trim milk,

no sugar please. I honestly look forward to getting up early because of my tea.
- A kiss on the lips from my love.

Two more senses

Most people know of our five physical senses, but there are two more: the sixth sense of intuition and the seventh sense of receiving. Some believe we actually have many more senses, but they are so subtle and esoteric that most of us cannot even grasp the concept. There is so much more that we don't know about life, don't you think?

To best accept the gifts of the sixth and seventh senses, we first need to be open to the possibility of their existence. As human beings we try to rationalise and analyse to help us understand. We cannot do this with the sixth and seventh senses; instead we need to trust and be receptive.

The sense of intuition

- Getting quiet so that you can hear your own responses to situations.
- Asking yourself instead of others if you have a question – everything you ever need to know is already inside of you – you only need to ask... and listen.
- Heeding your gut if you get a feeling. Asking yourself 'how am I feeling right now?' or '*what* am

I feeling right now?' then identifying where that feeling resides in your body. Is it a tightness in your chest? A heavy feeling in your stomach? An ache in your lower back? What do you think it means?

- Acting on your desires. Some believe that your desires are present for a reason, that they are there to lead you to where you are meant to go – much like a signpost on the road. I've also heard it said that if you have a particular desire, it's absolutely possible for you to have that desire in your life, otherwise you wouldn't have it. This way of thinking resonates, giving me the faith and confidence to continue towards my interests and passions.
- If you get a hunch and a good feeling, do something about it straight away – even if it's only a little research and a few notes to follow up – that five minutes could lead you somewhere amazing.
- Having gratitude for everything you have and everything that has happened to you. Even the bad times have shaped you to be the person you are today. This thought makes me feel better about my life. Sometimes I look back at the mistakes I've made or how someone's treated me badly; but it's all unfolding exactly as it should. I take comfort in that and, in the future do my best to be a good person.
- Practice picking up on individuals' vibes. Be open to the possibility and let them demonstrate themselves to you. I love to deal with people in a

simple, open and honest way. More and more I try not to have preconceptions about someone but simply let them show me who they are.

- Be open. When you stand up straight with good posture, your solar plexus which is often an area that feels tight and closed, will physically open up. A few deep breaths picturing this area opening will help your intuitive abilities. It feels good too, even if you don't believe in any of the other stuff.
- Be aware of your energy at different times of the month, being gentle with yourself when you're feeling more delicate. The more I do this the more I pick up. Our sixth sense of intuition is subtle, we can easily railroad and ignore it. Much like a quiet friend who has lots of wisdom to share, we gain much by listening and, much like a quiet friend, if we ignore it, it sits in the background being drowned out by the rowdier friends (us!).
- Be detached from outcomes. This has helped me find so much peace. I can want, ask and plan for something then the next step that helps the most is to let it go. What is meant to happen will happen. I don't use this as an excuse not to take action or make an effort, but there's a difference between making things happen and trying to force things to happen. I heard a great analogy: it's the difference between allowing a flower to open, and pulling the petals open. Surrender to the Universe's divine plan, because the Universe knows what's best for us (sometimes it's even better than what we've

come up with). Similar to a car's headlights at night, we can only see a little way in front of us and judge from that. The Universe however, can see our entire journey, right to the end. Trust that everything will work out exactly as it should, because it always does.

- Ground yourself, literally. Put both feet flat on the floor and feel yourself drawing up energy from the earth (even if you are inside). When I do this my feet sometimes tingle. I also love to lie on my back on the floor. Imagine the floor supporting you; it's okay to sink into it and let it hold you up. A few minutes is quite refreshing. I like to lie with my arms in a stop sign position but you can put them down beside you too (with palms facing up). I learned this from my yoga class – the teacher told us to 'let the floor support you'. It feels wonderful.

The sense of receiving

- When someone offers you praise or a compliment, accept it sincerely with a simple thank you.
- Accept help from others without batting them away. An example could be when my husband offers to help me with something and I'd automatically say 'no thanks, it's fine, I can do it'. It's hard for me to accept his help for some reason, but when I respond instead with 'thank you, that would be great', the sky doesn't fall in. Because he works more hours out of the home than I do, I feel

like I should do more at home than he does. But if he's happy to help and we get to chat while we complete a job, there's no downside.

- Asking others for help. Because I like to feel independent and not in debt to anyone, it's rare that I would ask for help unless I really can't do something myself. I never want to be one of those people that others are fearful of what they're going to be asked to do next, so I'm the complete opposite. I'm sure I do let opportunities slip by though, where others would happily help out, because that's what family and friends do, right? I've also heard that asking someone to help you makes the other person feel useful, so as long as it's not a task that could prove onerous or difficult, why not?
- Accepting your financial worth, not brushing off payment as unimportant. Be happy to ask for what you think you're worth. In our retail store I often think I should discount items people are buying because they are nice or I've seen them around so feel like I know them. They have brought an item to the counter intending to pay for it so why would I think like that? Artists, writers and crafty types are also notorious for undercharging. With something like a painting, you can charge what you like, but it should at least cover the costs of your materials and time, then think about all the hours of training and practice you've had. It's true that an item is only worth what someone is willing to pay,

but it's also true that people can subconsciously be suspicious of something that is too cheap. They may wonder why, asking themselves if there is anything wrong with it. High pricing is sometimes used as a marketing strategy too, which is an interesting concept.

- Instead of *giving* to charity, think of it as *gifting*, then receive a good feeling in return instead of begrudgement that giving can sometimes feel like.
- Along the same lines, instead of *taking*, think of it as *receiving*. Picture yourself *taking* a deep breath then *receiving* a deep breath. It feels totally different and more effortless too – receiving doesn't come from a place of neediness like taking does. It's absolutely fascinating just how different the feeling is.

Thirty Chic Days inspirational ideas:

What would **your own version of these lists** look like? You might like some of my examples so you could write those down to get the ball rolling, then think about what would make you feel joyous and prickling with golden glitter on the inside.

Once you get started, creating your own sensuous living lists is such fun and will provide inspiration for the future. Don't feel self-conscious, **do it just for you**.

Bonus Day
Take inspired action

To live a truly blessed and chic life, there's one step that is the most important and it's to *take inspired action*. This is the step which brings us closer to our goals and dreams – every little step counts.

What you are doing, *right now*, is either carrying you closer to your dream, or taking you further away from it – there is no in-between. If, like me, you are the type who thinks about things a lot, makes plans, compiles lists in a notebook; spending a lot of time in your head rather than in the real world, you will find it a tonic to stop thinking and take action.

Doing this cures all sorts of malaise and it is so refreshing – it sounds odd to say the cure is to 'do something' but it is. I need constant reminders when I'm thinking too much and feeling anxious because I'm not achieving anything. I am a champion daydreamer, but until I actually *do something* my life stays the same. Wishing and hoping won't achieve much either.

I might dream of the perfect capsule wardrobe (*be still my heart*) and think how good my closet would look with a serious pruning, but if my continued actions are to open the closet door, think it looks like too much work and not do anything, nothing changes.

Strike while the iron is hot

Brian Tracy said when you hear an idea that resonates, you will either do something about it straight away or you will *never* do anything about it; therefore, his message is to 'strike while the iron is hot'. I have certainly found this to be true.

Before hearing his words, a brilliant notion would come to me and I'd think 'what a great idea!', but my next thought would always be 'I have a lot on my plate right now, so I'll put that on my ideas list'. Of course you know where that got me; I never acted on the thought so my genius idea is still languishing in a notebook somewhere. Energy is always freshest at the time of the lightning bolt, so I now make the most of it.

Since hearing Brian's message, I act more often on an impulse which has had fantastic results. For the most part these little detours have slotted in with what I'm already doing so I don't lose much time. To be honest it probably *replaced* time where I was mucking around doing not much at all so I didn't lose, in fact I gained. In addition, the momentum and self-worth I gathered from completing these projects was invaluable.

So may I respectfully suggest you act immediately on your ideas and see how quickly you move forward.

Fortune favours action

If I feel stuck, I take a moment to list all the things I want to do or, alternatively, all the things that are bothering me. I then have it out of my head and onto paper with a concrete plan to work through. I don't have to do everything all at once; I can either choose the most important action if it's time-critical, the one that seems easiest to start, or even the one that looks the most fun simply to get me moving.

Often it's *starting* that is the hardest part. I heard the beautiful, late Jackie Collins say in an interview that she didn't have writer's block, she had 'getting to the desk' block.

For me it's the same with housework. I don't have resistance to housework, I have resistance to *starting* housework – getting out the vacuum cleaner, the paper towels, the cleaning spray. Once I'm going I carry on happily.

Filing paperwork in the office is another task I have trouble starting. Facing that stack of papers is not a good feeling but once I start going through it, punching holes and putting papers in their rightful place, it's actually quite meditative; seeing order restored from mess is very satisfying.

Often I'll walk past a small pile of something, notice it and at the same time wish it wasn't there. If I don't pick it up no-one is else is likely to, especially if I'm the only one home at the time, so why not do something about it the first time I notice it? It can be days or even weeks that a folded newspaper article can lie on our dining table. Moving that article to my magazine reading stack would be a start – it's off the table and in the right place for me to pick up next time I'm looking for something to read.

Do something huge

I did this by self-publishing. For many years I dreamt of writing and being a published author; I'd start writing a novel then tell myself 'people will think this is rubbish' and put it away. The bug was always there though so I'd start another book only to do the same thing.

When I started my blog I had a secret hope that an editor or book publishing company would read it and email me saying 'you're amazing, we want you to write for us!' That hasn't happened yet... but you never know.

One day I read a book where the author mentioned that she'd self-published and how easy it is to do these days. She said self-publishing used to have a stigma; it used to be that you weren't good enough for a real publishing company. Nowadays even many established authors are choosing to self-publish as well as new authors getting the chance to offer their work to the public.

So I did something about it, I researched how to self-publish and I started. There was no downside – it wasn't costing me a huge amount of money to investigate, only my time. I thought to myself, *What's the worst that can happen? I write a book and no-one likes it?* I can live with that. And at the end of this process I've written a book. That's something to be proud of.

Another big change we're thinking of making is a lifestyle change – moving out of the city to a small town where the pace of life is slower. I've been dreaming of this for a long time, even before I met my husband in fact. Thankfully he loves the idea too, so we're planning to make this our reality within the next couple of years.

Do you have a dream that you are afraid to acknowledge? Do you need to take massive, scary, unprecedented action and launch it out there? Or is there something you secretly want to look into that you can take baby steps towards and see what happens?

I've come to realise that *you* need to back yourself before anyone else will. You need to choose what you want to do, no-one else should have that privilege (unless you want to live a life that someone else thinks is best for you).

You don't need to tip your life upside down though; simply start taking small steps towards your big, scary desire. You can then course-correct along the way as you see what feels good and what doesn't. Set your plans in sand, rather than stone.

Something worth remembering is that *you are always free to change your mind*. Just because you have made the decision to do something doesn't mean you have to carry on with it for the rest of your days. Don't let the thought of 'what if I end up not liking this?' stop you from looking into a secret dream you have.

Thirty Chic Days inspirational ideas:

Make a commitment to yourself that the next time you have a thunderbolt idea, you'll take immediate action towards implementing it. If it's a small task you can then enjoy the rewards of both completion and something new in your life. It might be something tiny, like rearranging daily-use items in your kitchen to make them easier to access. If it's a bigger task, set out a plan then take the first step; you will feel the excitement of having something wonderful in the works.

Take the time to **daydream about your secret desires** and wonder how you could bring them into your life. Suspend reality while you do this to see where your mind takes you. If there were no limitations or consequences, what would you like to be, have or do? Ask yourself, '*how could I...?*'

Choose the chapter that resonates most with you in *Thirty Chic Days* and take action on a few ideas within it. Have fun with this; feel your anticipation and delight rise to the surface, like fine bubbles in a chilled glass of Perrier. *Santé* (cheers) to you!

Acknowledgments

A huge thank you to Rose Marshall for her assistance in editing *Thirty Chic Days*, with special thanks to my dear friend Karen M. Leong for her proofreading skills.

About the Author

Fiona Ferris is passionate about, and has studied the topic of living well for more than twenty years, in particular that a simple and beautiful life can be achieved without spending a lot of money.

Fiona finds inspiration from all over the place including Paris and France, the countryside, big cities, fancy hotels, music, beautiful scents, magazines, books, all those fabulous blogs out there, people, pets, nature, other countries and cultures; really everywhere she looks.

Fiona lives in beautiful Auckland, New Zealand, with her husband, Paul, and their two rescue cats Jessica and Nina.

To learn more about Fiona, you can connect with her at:

howtobechic.com
fionaferris.com
facebook.com/fionaferrisauthor
twitter.com/fiona_ferris
instagram.com/fionaferrisnz
youtube.com/fionaferris

Made in the USA
San Bernardino, CA
31 July 2016